EUCHARIST
Celebrating Its Rhythms in Our Lives

EUCHARIST
Celebrating Its Rhythms in Our Lives

Paul Bernier, sss

AVE MARIA PRESS   Notre Dame, Indiana 46556

© 1993 by Ave Maria Press, Notre Dame, IN 46556

International Standard Book Number: 0-87793-505-X (pbk.)
0-87793-506-8

Library of Congress Catalog Card Number: 92-75342

Cover and text design by Katherine Robinson Coleman.

Printed and bound in the United States of America.

To my mother,
whose death
as these thoughts were being written
closes the rhythms of earthly life to begin the eternal.

Contents

Preface

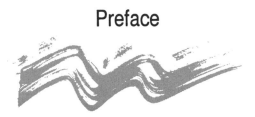

The Vatican Council called the eucharist the "source and summit of Christian life." It is a beautiful statement. But it is simply not true. It can be justified theologically, but the facts of the matter are quite otherwise. The vast majority of the Christian world—and the Catholic world as well—doesn't believe it at all. Christians do not celebrate it with any regularity and do not see it as providing much direction for understanding their lives.

Some church leaders indict those who do not celebrate regularly as having little fervor. More likely, they are simply demonstrating that the celebration provides no essential link between the liturgy and their daily lives. Their faith and belief in Christ is such that the eucharistic celebration plays but a minor role.

It should also be noted that, on another level, official church policy itself does not go out of its way to give primary emphasis to making the eucharist accessible. More importance is placed on maintaining an elite, all-male priesthood than on ordaining a sufficient number of people to remain a eucharistic church. Ecclesiastical policies that set stringent or arbitrary requirements for priesthood help to perpetuate situations where large numbers of people have no real access to the eucharist. This says, at the practical level, that church law and discipline are more important than eucharist for Christian life.

Be that as it may, there is no doubt that a gap has developed between everyday Christian life and the eucharist. It is not seen as the source and summit of Christian life as much as a devotion, as something optional. Hence, the purpose of this book: to try to bridge the gap between liturgy and daily life, so that the inner reality and dynamism of the eucharist itself begin to inspire the self-understanding of the Christian.

Underlying the approach of this book is a theology of eucharist that differs somewhat from the devotional understanding that fills many spiritual books. It also differs from theological approaches that are inspired more by scholastic theology than by the scriptures. We do not wish to deny any value in these approaches, but they will not solve the problems of our times.

We need a new approach. Unless a better way is found of explaining the eucharist, we are in danger of reinforcing a piety that is becoming less and less meaningful for a great number of people and that may even have been set aside by the theology of Vatican II. If our celebrations and catechesis do not keep this in mind, the eucharist will be no more than an external display with no lasting effects.

Two major emphases underlie the approach of this book. The first is a conviction that we must move from a devotional (private, individualistic) understanding of eucharist to a communal one. Second, we must go from a passive to an active appreciation of the meaning of this (and, indeed, every) sacrament.

We know that by the thirteenth century communion at least once a year had to be made a matter of church law. This shows the extent to which people had fallen from liturgical practice and an understanding of the role of the eucharist in Christian life. Whether they felt unworthy to receive communion because of a sense of personal sinfulness or simply lacked appreciation of the meaning of the liturgy, the eucharist had little effective influence in people's lives. They turned instead to devotions of various kinds. These gave them more immediate contact with the divine, especially because the saints seemed closer, somehow, to the everyday world than the church's liturgy.

Eventually the eucharist itself became another devotion. This was the era of processions, expositions of the blessed sacrament, of people running from church to church in order to catch another moment of consecration. Examples could easily be multiplied. The fact remains, however, that the eucharistic devotions tended to lose their rootedness in the liturgy. The consequence was further to divorce the "source and summit" of people's lives from the reality of their everyday world.

One major problem with the devotional approach is that it ignores the communal dimension of the eucharist. It becomes a private, individualistic relationship with Jesus rather than an ecclesial one. Saying that the eucharist is the source and summit of Christian life is meant to express the conviction of the Fathers, who affirmed that it was the eucharist that made the church. However, statements such as these will remain but pious hopes unless eucharist is seen as the action of the entire Christian community gathered to express its identity.

Interestingly, one of the first names given the eucharist in the New Testament is *ekklesia*, "church." For the early community, the theology and understanding of what it meant to be church and to gather for eucharist were one and the same. Even today we have been reminded by the *Constitution on the Sacred Liturgy*, as well as Pope Paul VI's encyclical *Mysterium fidei*, that there are other real presences of Christ in the church. One of the chief ones is his presence in the assembly gathered in his name to proclaim the liberation he has wrought by his death and resurrection, and the communion that should result from our being able to gather at the table of the Lord.

We also come to eucharist to be missioned, to continue the work of Christ. It may be possible to do this if we regard the eucharist as the highest and greatest of devotions. But ignoring the fact that eucharist is actually the public worship of all God's people does nothing to give us a proper sense of identity. Neither does it liberate the individual from private seclusion and give the sense of mission that comes from realizing our responsibilities as part of the new covenant people.

The symbolism of a community gathered by the Lord is a powerful reminder that we are called to continue the work of establishing the kingdom for which Jesus lived and died. This is what it means to be church.

Until recent years the communion rails effectively segregated the congregation from what was happening in the sanctuary. The impression given was that all the important actions took place there—and that there was no room for the people. Lectors and eucharistic ministers are very recent. The distinction between clergy and laity was so visibly emphasized in our churches that people naturally felt they really had no role to play in the liturgical action. Conversely, the liturgy had little role to play in their lives.

What, then, were people to do? If they went to church at all, it was mainly to receive something from God. They went to deepen their relationship with Jesus, or to receive grace, or to be enlightened. Perhaps they even looked forward to communion and the sacramental encounter that it permitted. But this essentially passive attitude makes it impossible really to enter into the eucharistic action, because we see it as belonging to someone else—to the priest, or to Jesus. We do not see it as *our* action as well. Thus the eucharistic prayer itself becomes an exercise in nostalgia or historical memory of what Jesus did for us almost two thousand years ago. However, if our sacramental encounter with the risen Lord is to have any meaning at all, it will be because Jesus meets us on our life's journey and invites us to join in solidarity with him, to become agents of the world's salvation.

"Do this in memory of me." We repeat these words at each eucharist. The tendency is to see them only as the words of the priest. Even worse, we think of them as applying solely to the words of consecration. But Jesus never asked us to repeat words. He asked us to *do* what he himself was doing at that moment. That was preparing to give his life for the salvation of the world. St. John's chapter 13 shows Jesus washing the feet of the disciples as an example of what we ourselves should be doing for one another. All in memory of him. Eucharist asks us to join with Jesus in the task of the world's salvation.

Eucharist is solidarity. Jesus invites us to his table that he might inspire us with his vision and join us with himself in the salvation of others. This is the missionary dimension of the church and eucharist. If our eucharists in the past have not been totally effective in transforming lives, in making the faithful more committed to the work of Christ, perhaps it is because people have felt they were there to receive rather than to give. The hands we have outstretched, however, are not only to receive the body of Christ; they are, in turn, to give him to others. This is the essence of Christian mission. And it belongs to the entire people by reason of baptism.

I am convinced of the theological truth that the eucharist is the source and summit of Christian life. I am also convinced of its practical falsity for the majority of Christian people. Perhaps years of passive and devotional eucharists have effectively isolated it from daily consciousness and life; eucharist says almost nothing about the real world of economics, politics, or social realities. Making eucharist and our relationship with Jesus private strikes at the root of the nature of the Christian community. We are a sacramental people, and a sacramental church—sacraments, that is, of the saving power of Christ.

The eucharist is a challenge to the church and to the world. Our common problems will be solved only when we can learn to love one another the way Jesus has loved us—love, incidentally, that can require even giving our lives for one another. Each time we celebrate eucharist, we proclaim the death of one who has given his life for us, and who looks to us to be willing to do the same. It is this active love and commitment that is at the heart of eucharist.

The approach to eucharist in this book, then, situates it at the heart of the church, expressive of what the church itself is; at the same time it helps to live out in our daily lives what we celebrate at the table of the Lord.

There is meant to be a reciprocity between liturgy and life. This reciprocity can be understood by looking more deeply into the basic rhythms that characterize the eucharistic liturgy. These are the very same rhythms meant to characterize the Christian community. The truth of this was borne home to me in a striking article by Edward Gabriele "The Ministry of the Eucharistic Presider" [*Emmanuel*, vol. 93 (April 1987), pp. 144-51]. His article provides the outline for this book.

Whether we recognize it or not, there *is* a reciprocity between liturgy and everyday life. That is, the effectiveness of our eucharists and the power of our Christian witness are directly related. It is impossible to celebrate the eucharist meaningfully if our lives are not eucharistic in the fullest sense of that term.

Furthermore, a well-celebrated eucharist has the ability to mold the community so that it becomes what Christ intended it to be: his true body. Before the twelfth century the body of Christ meant the church. The church and the *corpus Christi eucharisticum* (or *mysticum*) were practically identified with each other. Since then, however, we have reversed our understanding and priorities. The body of Christ has come to mean the eucharist, and the mystical body the church. Furthermore, we have come to see the church as a divinely instituted hierarchical organization with the eucharist as one of the several means of grace dispensed by it for the growth of individual members.

We have to realize that the eucharist is not what the church *does*; it is what the church *is*. The identity of the church as the body of Christ is both expressed and effectively proclaimed by its being centered in the reality of his body and blood. Thus the ancient dictum of the Fathers: it is not only the eucharist that makes the church, it is the church that makes the eucharist.

1

Learning God's Dance

I danced in the morning
when the world was begun,
And I danced in the moon
and the stars and the sun.
And I came down from heaven
and I danced on the earth.
At Bethlehem I had my birth.

Some fifty years ago Sydney Carter wrote the modern arrangement of an old Shaker hymn called "The Lord of the Dance." It is unusual in that it pictures God as master of the cosmic dance of creation. The One who has danced in the moon and the stars and the sun was also born in Bethlehem to dance on the earth. In his goodness he offers to let us share in his dance, and he will lead us all, wherever we might be.

The imagery here captures perfectly what true Christian life is all about: learning to dance to God's tune. Christian life is not doing our own thing, or dancing our own dance. We are not alone in the dance. It was first learned and danced to perfection by Jesus, who was one with God and in harmony with all of creation. Its varied steps are spelled out in the scriptures. Even better, the essence of this melody is repeated for us over and over again in the Sunday liturgy. Eucharist is the tune of the one who danced even on the Friday when the sun turned black as he hung on the cross. For he is the life that will never, never die. His greatest desire is to live again in us so that the dance may go on.

For years we tended to think of the sacraments as things. Each was thought of in terms of a special grace, which we received from it. Vatican II has reminded us that the sacraments are liturgical actions, not things. *Eucharist*, for example, is an action of the church gathered together, not something done by the priest. If we ever thought of the sacraments as actions of the church previously, it was because they were dispensed in and by the church. However, the *Constitution on the Sacred Liturgy* reminds us that "the full and active participation of all the people is the aim to be considered before all else" (no. 14).

As actions, it is helpful to think of the liturgy as a dance God invites us to join. We are affected by what we do. To speak of the liturgy as a dance is to realize that it is God who pipes the tune, who sets the basic rhythms. For each of us the dance will be different, reflecting the differences in our bodies, our lives, our relationships. This can be a frightening thought for those who prefer a clear-cut pattern, a uniform set of steps that all of us must dance.

However, there is really no fixed form we all must observe. We are not asked to mimic Jesus' steps, although we are to be inspired by his music. We need to let this speak to us and inspire us to dance as Jesus did, filled with his own Spirit. The question is not what Jesus himself might have danced were he alive today. We really don't know. Rather, we need to ask how we might be to people today what Jesus was to people in his own time. This is learning to dance to the same tune that Jesus did, a tune that comes from God. And though its basic rhythms are the same, the steps will differ depending on the circumstances of time and place.

In the modern world in which we live, the main thing that will sustain us in life's dance is the liturgy. There, in a world where improvisation is a virtue, we can hear the rhythms that ought to control our lives. Without this, we will lose the beat, forget the melody, or mistake the rhythm. Only in the liturgy do all of life's rhythms come together. Without liturgy, we are left with little to fall back on.

It is said that Catholics are a sacramental people. What does this really mean? Only that Catholics tend to stress and celebrate the sacraments more frequently than others? And how does one celebrate the sacraments meaningfully? Is sharing in the church's sacraments something like getting a dividend on religious practice? Perhaps storing up merit in some supernatural bank account? Or is it a special way of thinking, a whole way of life?

Unfortunately, most people continue to think of sacraments as something we receive rather than something we *do*. What is the relationship between the lives that we lead and the sacraments that we celebrate? Do our lives have any effect on the sacraments? Consider the following three situations.

My secretary shared this story with me one Monday morning. Her husband had gone to a wedding the previous Saturday in a small town some thirty miles away. At the reception the bride took the glass of champagne and announced, "I want to make the toast." Raising her glass she continued, "To my husband—the first and last day of our marriage!" With that she threw the champagne in his face and walked majestically out of the hall.

As everyone stood with mouths agape, wondering what had happened, it was learned that the previous night the bride-to-be had discovered that her beloved had been unfaithful to her. Such was her anger that, rather than simply call off the wedding, she preferred to embarrass him in front of all his friends. Everyone agreed that she succeeded spectacularly.

Think back, however, to the hour before the reception, when all were gathered in church. There, when the priest asked whether she took the person at her side as her husband and she answered yes while all the while her heart was saying no, no, no!, what was actually being celebrated?

Or take the case of a person who comes to confession during Holy Week, not having confessed for a whole year. He mentions adultery. Actually, he has a mistress. When I say, "I suppose you have been coming here year after year at this time to receive absolution. Then, after receiving communion on Easter you go right back to your mistress?" "That's right," he answers.

If, despite there being no real sorrow or purpose of amendment, I go ahead and give absolution anyway, what actually would be celebrated?

Take a third case. We have a community that is divided, where there are factions, where the rich are not ashamed to ignore the poor. Yet they all gather to celebrate a magnificent eucharist. The singing is perfect, the vestments superb, the presider inspired. What is really being celebrated?

We have an authoritative answer to this last case. It was given by St. Paul himself. He said something like, "I don't know what on earth you think you are celebrating, but it surely isn't the eucharist!" (cf. 1 Cor 11:20).

What was being celebrated, we might add, was selfishness, division, and sin. That surely is not the eucharist.

These examples are meant as graphic illustrations of the fact that there is nothing magic about the sacraments. They don't work automatically, despite a lack of love or faith on our part. We can't share in a sacrament and expect to be graced if our lives contradict the very meaning of the sacrament that we are celebrating. Some theologians speak of split-level Christianity, a situation where prayer has no seeming influence on values, ideals, or lifestyle. This is sham Christianity, sham sacraments. There is meant to be a close relationship between liturgy and life. We are expected to dance to God's tune at all times.

In actuality, the relationship between the sacraments and life is a reciprocal one. In other words, sacraments influence our lives (perhaps less rather than more) and our lives influence our celebration of the sacraments (surely more rather than less). St. Paul is a frightening reminder that our lives can be such that they completely vitiate what we think we are celebrating. Sacraments are celebrations of the reality of our lives.

Though the sacraments, and especially the eucharist, are primarily worship, they are also expected to influence our practice and mold our thinking—to turn us into Christians in fact as well as in name. Celebration of eucharist is meant to make us eucharistic in thought, word, and deed. The liturgy is an experience that demands a personal involvement on our part, a response to the action of Christ. It is a font of formation in true Christian imagination. It helps us to think and act as Christians.

What is celebrated at the altar is meant to be paralleled in actual life. What we live out daily is what is brought to the altar to be transformed by God. But, as the eminent liturgist Robert Hovda wryly notes, just as we can't get blood out of a turnip, we can't expect to have warm, experiential liturgical celebrations with an unconcerned people, those who have no interest in the economic and political oppression and division that exists in our world. God will not dance to our tune.

A true Christian spirit is a eucharistic spirit. The Sunday liturgy and our efforts to discern the signs of our times provide the basic material with which Christian life is built. This implies some sort of organic unity in our lives, a wholeness, so that our daily existence can be shaped by our faith, especially by its liturgical expression. Eucharistic rhythms reveal the rhythms of Christian life.

Granted this is easier said than done. It is not a simple thing to become versed in the language of our worship. Many liturgies suffer from symbolic minimalism and shoddy practice. Further, because we do not yet have a truly vernacular liturgy, the elements that go into making up our present rites do not always combine to engage our senses and imagination, indeed the whole of our being, as they should. Consequently, few develop a truly eucharistic spirituality.

A lot can still happen on the subliminal level, however. As mentioned earlier, Catholics are said to be a sacramental people. Some feel we carry the sacramental principle to an extreme. Yet, there is such a thing as the Catholic imagination. We are prone to seeing created realities as being able to speak to us of God. We use bread and wine, people gathering for a common meal, oil and water, statues, and rosaries as ways of expressing our belief that God can and does touch the common clay of our daily lives to invest them with the presence of the divine.

This involves a unique way of looking at life and reality. We might note two basic ways of looking at the world in which we live. We can see it as being either fundamentally good or as something evil. Those who are more impressed by the injustice and the pain, the sin and the sorrow of life, are faced with a universe that seems basically corrupt. They see the world as a somewhat God-forsaken place, antagonistic to true life in the Spirit. Redemption then becomes a problem. Seemingly, no matter what Jesus was able to accomplish personally, nothing has really changed for us. The world is still evil, we are still depraved, and the Holy Spirit has a mighty struggle to get us to cooperate with God's grace.

We might characterize this as the radical Protestant position. It expresses a strong realization of the reality of sin and its consequences, realities that mar the beauty of God's creation and render it a temptation on life's road. There are innumerable practical consequences of this attitude. Protestant churches, for example, tend to reject the "smells and bells" of Catholicism. There are no statues, and little ornamentation. Everything reflects a very sober austerity.

The Catholic instinct, however, is otherwise. The Catholic intuition is to take the creation stories of Genesis rather literally, not so much as an account of actual events, but in the realization that after each of the days of creation, God was able to look back with pride on his work and say that it was good. Everything in the world up to and including Adam's ability to look at the naked Eve and thank God that she was bone of his bone and flesh of his flesh was—and is—good.

This complicates accounting for the evil that is also an obvious part of our world. But this is the fault of humankind itself, not of the God who is present to his creatures and who reveals himself in and through the created world. All of creation can therefore speak to us of God. Thus was St. Francis brought closer to God by Brother Sun and Sister Moon. The work of redemption wrought by Christ is, in the Catholic mind, something intrinsic. By making us his children, God has changed us, ennobled us, filled us with his Spirit.

This is why the world can in a very real sense be a sacrament of God. It continues to speak of his goodness and love, as well as his compassion and concern for his creation. And so we are a sacramental people; we see ourselves as deprived rather than depraved, focus more on community, are less individualistic in religious practice, and can enjoy the laughter and good red wine for which Hilaire Belloc praised God.

This sacramental sense is seldom adverted to. But it is there nonetheless. If it becomes more conscious, however, perhaps we might find it easier to integrate our life and our worship. We can in this way develop a more holistic spirituality. In stressing the basic rhythms that characterize our ritual, we can dance better to these same rhythms. This means looking afresh at our lives and asking in what way they might more clearly reflect the underlying rhythms of the eucharist.

The approach taken here may appear a bit simplistic. For the sake of the presentation we can seemingly ignore or pass over the wealth of the entire liturgy to focus only on its component parts. However, in speaking of the entrance rite in terms of the gathering rhythm, we do not mean to imply that the community dimension is found nowhere else. Likewise, when stressing how God's word forms and challenges the people who hear it, there is no need to assume that this is found only in the liturgy of the word. God's word is most active during the eucharistic prayer.

Our highlighting of the various parts of the rite are intended to isolate the basic rhythms that characterize them as well as the entire liturgy. It is hoped that this will enable us to get a better feel for the liturgy itself, for the recurring rhythms of the life it offers us. This will allow us to examine our relationships, our involvements, to see how they might more clearly attest to the underlying beat of our prayer and praise.

Thus, what we are examining here goes beyond specific practices or programs of spirituality to focus on a way of thinking—a way of thinking that will inform our entire lives. Our various styles of life will continue to be different, just as the circumstances that surround us are different. It is the Holy Spirit who gives us many gifts, thereby calling us to life and inviting us each to the dance.

The five rhythms of the eucharistic celebration are intrinsic to the liturgy. They are as follows:

The *gathering* rhythm. Before anything begins, the liturgy is the story of God gathering people together from every race and nation. The Christian community is one where there is no longer Jew nor Greek, slave nor free, male nor female, but where all are one in Christ Jesus. This community or social dimension is not only an aspect of our worship, it is a characteristic of Christianity itself. As Tertullian said almost two thousand years ago, *"unus Christianus, nullus Christianus"* ("a solitary Christian is no Christian").

Then there is the *storytelling* rhythm. Someone once reduced the liturgical rhythms to three: gather the folks,

tell the stories, share the food. This seems a bit reduc-
tionist. Yet there is no doubt that we are people of the
story—not simply people who love to hear stories, but
people whose whole self-understanding is based on the
story of God's own self-revelation to us in the scriptures.
The Christian myth is basic to our appreciation of who
we are and what God wants us to be.

The third rhythm is the *prophetic* one. God's word
is not meant merely to inform or to console. It is meant
to stir us to dance God's dance, not our own. An important element in the liturgy of the word is the ever-
present challenge to get the world in which we live to
dance God's dance as well. God never intended for us
to be changed by the world in which we live, but rather
to change that world so that people might dwell in a
place stamped with more of the marks of the kingdom.

The fourth is the *nurturing* rhythm. We can well
associate this with the communion rite. The one thing
we should always remember is that God feeds us only
that we might have something with which to feed one
another. The church itself is meant to be a nurturing
community. In any community, where all are brothers
and sisters, the needs of one are the concern of all.

The final and most neglected rhythm may well be
the *missioning* rhythm. The proper function of our worship is to form our lives so that we might go forth and
be witnesses in the world of God's action in our lives.
The entire church is missioned to bring the good news
of Christ to the world. The image of the world that we
get in the Book of Revelation is one where all of creation
is dancing the cosmic dance of God. It is the task of
Christians to help bring this about and to realize that the
most important element of Christianity is not saving

one's soul as much as saving the souls of others, allowing God to use us to teach the world his dance.

It should be evident that we are not fostering a concrete way of life as much as a way of thinking and looking at life itself—learning the very dance of God. The rhythms of that dance embrace everything that we are and have. They indicate to us the concrete spirituality that should be ours in any given time and place. They make it possible for us—after the injunction of St. Paul—to offer our bodies as a living sacrifice to God (Rom 12:1-2).

According to Paul, this will occur only when we are no longer conformed to the spirit of this age, but have discerned what is the will of God, what is good and pleasing and perfect. This will not happen all at once. However, if we pattern our life's journey after the liturgy of the church, we will become transformed slowly into the fullness of Christ and be enabled to offer perfect worship to God. This type of spiritual worship is possible only when we are dancing to the rhythms that the Spirit of God herself dances and hopes that each of us will follow.

2

The Gathering Rhythm

I danced for the scribe
and the pharisee.
But they would not dance
and they wouldn't follow me.
I danced for the fishermen,
for James and John—
They came with me
and the dance went on.

The entrance rite is seldom considered a very important part of the liturgy. In fact, it didn't even exist until well into the fifth century. Until then the presider simply entered and everything began with the liturgy of the word. Very simple. Neat. No clutter.

Naturally the liturgy has to begin somewhere. But for the past fifteen-hundred years there have been various sorts of entrance rites. These serve several purposes. For one, they are an invitation to prayer, readying us for the solemn worship that is to follow. They also serve to welcome the community that is gathered. Wherever we prefer to put the emphasis, one point should be clear. On Sundays, perhaps the most important event that takes place is the gathering of the community to share in Christ's own sacrificial meal.

It is easy to skip over this fact and concentrate on the liturgical action whereby we are fed at both the table of Christ's word and of his flesh. Central to a proper understanding of the eucharist, however, is a proper appreciation for the significance of the community that gathers for the celebration.

A community is not the same thing as a mob. The Sunday assembly differs (or *should* differ) from a group of people at a sports event or a movie. There, all are doing the same thing at the same time. But they are doing it as individuals. They are together like marbles in a bag—cold, unfeeling, and uncaring about the others who may be there. The Christian community is not meant to be an amorphous mass of spectators, passively watching the action in the sanctuary.

Since the Second Vatican Council much stress has been placed on the community dimension of the eucharist. It may seem to some that we are trying to recapture a long-lost and unmourned ideal. In the first few centuries each city had only one church, and all the members could join together at the one and only mass that would be celebrated that day. They knew each other by name, and this knowledge moved into mutual care and concern.

The situation in our large cities, where most Christians are found, is far different. Churches are huge and characterized by many services. People don't really know one another. Not only is a sense of natural community hard to achieve, but many people aren't interested in achieving it. They relish the anonymity city life brings. And they don't see that community has anything to do with being able to assist profitably at mass.

This isolation is more than a sociological problem, however. It has acquired a (questionable) theological pedigree as well. Unfortunately, it reflects a theology that has been growing since the Middle Ages, when the liturgy was so incomprehensible that the vast majority of people were reduced to devising devotions of their own to nourish their piety.

Rather than focus on the community gathered at the Lord's table, there was a tendency to put the main emphasis on the mysterious presence of Jesus in the bread and the wine. Even today we judge the mass in terms of what happens to the bread and the wine—all of which hinges on having a validly ordained priest and using proper matter and form. This is a modern problematic. The early church focused instead on what happens to the people who share bread and wine in memory of Christ. Again, the emphasis was on people, and on the active dimension of coming together to celebrate our faith.

In the Middle Ages, however, especially after the elevation was introduced in the thirteenth century, the emphasis shifted. A lively reverence for the mystery that took place at the consecration developed. As mentioned before, some people would even go from church to church to catch the elevation of the host, which as often as not was shown to those gathered in the plaza for that purpose.

With this emphasis on the presence of Christ (the feast of Corpus Christi was instituted at this time), churches began to be understood in a different way. Originally a gathering place for the assembly, churches became the dwelling place of God. The growing devotion to Christ present in the tabernacle cemented this. Of course, the practice of visits to the blessed sacrament answered a very real need. People sensed the necessity of having a personal relationship with Jesus. Since the liturgy is essentially the public prayer of the community, there is little time provided for private prayer.

Hence, time spent before the tabernacle before or after the celebration helps to interiorize what has been celebrated at the altar.

The fact remains, nonetheless, that during the celebration of the eucharist, the tabernacle is a liturgical embarrassment. We are instructed to give it reverence if we pass it on entering or leaving. Otherwise, it is to be ignored. All attention should be focused on the altar and the ambo. The best solution seems to be having a special blessed sacrament chapel. This characterized many of the earlier churches, and provided an oasis of peace and calm that facilitated personal prayer.

Most of us have grown up with the expectation that this peace and calm was meant to be characteristic of the entire church. Hence the resistance when people are asked to greet one another at the beginning of the mass. There seems something vaguely Protestant to most Catholics about entering the church and finding people talking to each other instead of kneeling in quiet for personal prayer.

This is not to discourage the idea of personal prayer. We all need to internalize the celebration of Christ's memorial by a prayer that makes of our whole lives a prolongation of our eucharists. That having been said, it must also be insisted that the time for this is mainly before or after the celebration. When gathered for the liturgy the main focus is on the community itself and what it is about to engage in.

In this regard let me share a story that I heard from Dom Helder Camara. It must be one of his favorites, because I have heard it from him more than once. It seems that when he was still bishop of Recife, one day thieves pried open the tabernacle in one of his churches. Since they were mainly after the gold vessels and ciboria, they dumped out the hosts in the mud outside the church. Worse, they trampled on them before leaving.

This act shocked the people, who decided that they should have a day of prayer in reparation for the sacrilege. They invited Dom Helder to come and pray with them and offer a few words. He spoke as follows: "My dear people. We are gathered here to make reparation for a sacrilege that has been committed in our church. People broke into the tabernacle and trampled the body of Christ into the mud outside the church. This has saddened us, and rightly so. But, my dear people, in our country Christ is daily trampled in the mud in the persons who make up his body, and no one sheds a tear."

St. Augustine would have agreed fully. In his 272nd sermon he said, "If you are the body of Christ and its members, it is your mystery which has been placed on the altar of the Lord. You receive your own mystery; you say 'Amen' to what you are." This notion of the body of Christ, a theology that goes back to St. Paul, is not central to most people today. Yet, it goes to the heart of what it means to be redeemed. Salvation involves more than simply accepting Jesus as our personal savior. There is no warrant in the scriptures for such an individualized notion of salvation. Rather, we are saved by being brought into a community that is alive with the Spirit of Christ.

In both the Old Testament and the New Testament God's will to save has been manifested in his choosing a *people*. God chose Abraham *and his descendants*. It was the entire people that Moses brought out of Egypt. With them God forged a special relationship, a covenant whereby they would be known as his people, and he would reveal his law to them and help them to know his ways. Salvation was social.

In each of the accounts of the institution of the eucharist that we have in the New Testament, we are reminded of this when the evangelists speak of the covenant in Christ's blood (Paul and Luke) or the blood of the covenant (Mark and Matthew). Christ's actions are seen as the inauguration of a new covenant foretold by Jeremiah (31:31-34)—a redemptive community in continuity with God's promises and actions in the past.

Paul's development of his body of Christ theology makes it clear that he is dealing with more than a metaphor. Rather, he posits an organic link between the members of the body and a dependence of each upon the other. When one hurts, all hurt. Each member has a part to play for the good of the whole. The gifts of the Spirit are not personal prerogatives, but given for the good of the entire body.

The term "in Christ," which Paul uses more than four dozen times, is another concrete example of how he understood God's grace to be mediated. The practical problem faced by Paul was how to get the Gentile converts to "put on the mind of Christ." This was rendered difficult because they came from an environment in which they were surrounded by pagan friends, neighbors, and relatives, whose values and behavior were thoroughly pagan.

For Paul, they could truly "convert" only if they lived "in Christ," by which he meant the Christian community that could mediate a new value system, provide new role models, people who could support one another with their example and help. It was *in the community* that a convert would encounter Christ. One was saved by Christ's death and rescued from the grasp of an evil age (cf. Gal 1:4) by becoming part of the caring community that formed Christ's body here on earth.

For the past few hundred years we have been influenced by a spiritual individualism that has had an insidious effect on our proper understanding of what the church is all about. It leads us to imagine God's reign as an interior reality in the souls of individual believers scattered over the face of the earth. However, it is not as individuals but precisely as a people that the church can be a credible sign of salvation to the rest of the world.

The Protestant Reformation made a deliberate effort to put people into direct contact with God. As a desire to free people from an often oppressive religious establishment, which seemed to claim a monopoly of the means of salvation, this was admirable. But when the influential theologian Adolf von Harnack approvingly described the last century as one of religious individualism and subjectivism, it was because he was convinced that this also accurately described Jesus' teaching.

According to Harnack, the kingdom of God comes by coming to *individuals*, making entrance into their souls and being grasped by them. The kingdom of God is the rule of God in individual hearts. In such an understanding we don't really need the church. It becomes only a fraternity of well-meaning people throughout the world. Christianity is then concerned only with the interior life; the social dimension of our faith becomes decidedly secondary.

To some extent we have all been influenced by this. Despite our retention of a generalized theology of community, we have managed to live it in a much more individualistic way than it was originally conceived. The seventeenth century laid enormous emphasis on developing a strong personal spirituality. Our pastoral practice and understanding of the church and its liturgy is still largely individualistic.

I can think of an incident, not too many years ago, that many will surely find familiar. It was a 7:00 A.M. mass, and there were about fifty people present. After entering the church I began with the usual, "In the name of the Father, and of the Son and of the Holy Spirit." No response. I continued, "The Lord be with you." Once again I was answered only with profound silence. As I looked around at the people who were scattered about the church, as far from each other as possible, I noticed some in the back lighting candles to St. Anne. Others had their noses buried in ancient prayer books. Still others were fingering a rosary, silently mouthing their prayers.

Somewhat provoked, I abandoned my prepared remarks for the homily. "I have only one question to ask you this morning," I said instead. "What are you doing here? Our faith tells us that when we gather for the eucharist we are all together at the banquet of the Lord. Here Jesus himself feeds us with his word and with his flesh. Yet, all of you seem to have brought your own lunch!"

Hearing of this, a friend suggested that I write an article entitled "Brownbagging It at the Table of the Lord." Flippant as this may sound, people do it every day. They go to church to do their own thing, not God's. This individualistic piety ignores one very important reality: the presence of Christ in the community.

The eucharistic presence does not take place in a vacuum. Rather, as the Vatican Council and Pope Paul VI (in both *Mysterium fidei* and in the *Instruction on Eucharistic Worship*) have made clear, it takes place within a whole network of interrelated ways in which Christ remains really present to us. In the liturgy we should be especially concerned with his presence in the priest, in the proclamation of the word, in acts of charity done in his name and in the bread and the wine. But, to begin with, he is present in those who have come together in his memory. "Where two or three of you are gathered together in my name, there I am in the midst of them" (Mt 18:20).

We must disabuse ourselves of the idea that Christ is somehow absent until the moment of consecration. An old French hymn used to express this quite graphically. It invited us to adore the gentle lamb and the bread of angels, who came down from heaven for us. Jesus doesn't need to "come down" from anywhere for us. He is already present to us in a number of ways, the most visible and powerful sign of that presence being the community that is gathered, especially when it is one in love and peace.

It is precisely this presence in the community—a fact which underlies the very nature of the Christian community—that every liturgy should help to reinforce. Gathering together each Sunday requires an active faith, an act of recognition on our part. We are called to recognize the presence of Christ in all who gather. It is because of his presence that there is no longer Jew nor Greek, slave nor free, male nor female. Rather, we are all one in Christ Jesus (cf. Gal 3:26-28).

This unity and oneness is something that we pray for in each eucharist when we ask the Holy Spirit to transform us so that we might "truly become one body, one spirit in Christ." This special prayer to the Holy Spirit has been introduced in all our new eucharistic prayers. In so doing, the church was only going back to the usage of the most ancient prayers of the church.

There the Holy Spirit was always asked to sanctify the church, to "bring us together in unity."

Unfortunately, the way this prayer has been presently crafted can obscure its meaning. It has been split in two. Just before the words of institution, we ask the Holy Spirit to "come upon the gifts to make them holy so that they may become for us the body and blood of our Lord, Jesus Christ." This causes us no problems. We are used to thinking of the mass as involving the transformation of bread and wine into the body and blood of Christ. We take it for granted that this will happen.

We can forget, however, the second part of the prayer. We are actually asking the Holy Spirit for a double transformation. We pray that the Spirit change both the elements on the altar *and those of us who are gathered to share them.* We explicitly ask that we be made one, just as Jesus prayed at the last supper (cf. John 17). We would be shocked if we were told that the Holy Spirit was not able to bring about the transformation of the gifts. We would think that this vitiated the whole mass. But what happens if the Spirit is unable to bring about the transformation of the community?

At the end of St. Paul's teaching on the eucharist in 1 Corinthians, he has the following pregnant sentence, "Anyone who eats and drinks without discerning the body, eats and drinks judgment on himself" (11:29). In Catholic circles there has been a tendency to see this as an insistence on our acknowledging the presence of Christ in the eucharistic elements. Or it is seen as inculcating a proper respect and behavior before that presence. Paul, however, is dealing not with the presence of Christ in the bread and the wine. He is insisting on Christ's presence in those who "meet as a church" (11:17).

The entire problem Paul addresses in chapter 11 is the failure to recognize Christ in those who have gathered and the consequent shaming of the poorer members of the community by the rich. Paul says that such a lack of recognition brings about not only judgment on ourselves, but can even vitiate the celebration. Indeed, recognition of the whole Christ, head and body, is the indispensable foundation for any proper and profitable celebration of eucharist. Only then do we sense the mystery that we are celebrating—a mystery whereby one who is absent becomes present in a world that otherwise conceals him.

This, then, is what the entrance rite of the mass should recall for us. It begins even before the opening hymn. In many churches we are greeted at the door. At times someone invites us to greet one another as the service is about to begin. But where this does not happen, it would be appropriate for us to somehow acknowledge the presence of those in the pew alongside us as we (or they) enter.

Then comes the badly named entrance hymn. The purpose of this hymn is not to mark time while the procession of ministers gets into the sanctuary. How many times do we hear something like, "Now let us rise to greet our celebrant . . ." The hymn is *not* to greet the priest or to get him to the altar. It's more a joyful gathering hymn, helping to set the mood of the day's celebration. We all join in because we are *all* celebrants. This is *our* liturgy. The priest leads or presides, but it is the whole body of Christ that offers common worship to God.

I am becoming less and less enchanted these days with those who begin the liturgy with a folksy, "Good morning!" I see nothing lacking with one of the more liturgical greetings. I have also been wondering of late

why the ancient *"Dominus vobiscum"* is always translated "The Lord be with you." After all, the Latin has no
verb. Why not "The Lord *is* with you"? Do we not
translate the similar greeting given by the angel to Mary
as "The Lord *is* with you"?

Perhaps we are able and willing to see the Lord as
truly being with someone like Mary, or with any obviously holy person. But when it comes to God being
with the person next to me, or even with oneself, this is
a more startling concept. It demands that we take our
dignity seriously, that we recognize that when we
gather in Christ's name we form his body. Jesus is truly
with us. Were it not so, we could never proceed to bring
about his presence in bread and wine.

The rubrics then allow the presider to give a short
introduction. It would take only one sentence to remind
us that we have come together as a body to worship the
Lord and to focus our attention on that day's liturgy.
Whatever form of penance rite is used, we are invited
to realize that our lives outside the church do make a
difference to our celebration. We have a responsibility
to one another. We are not there alone.

The entrance rite ends with an invitation to prayer,
"Let us pray." The pause here is not to give us a chance
to look around and get distracted. It is to allow us to
plug ourselves into this particular celebration, in this
time and place. Wherever we are on life's journey, we
ask God to be able to sink our lives more fully into
Christ's. We acknowledge that he is our God, asking
that we be more attentive to his dance. The priest then
sums up all our personal prayers in the opening prayer,
and we are ready to listen again to the wonderful story
of our salvation.

3

With Open Hearts: Solidarity in Christ

David and all Israel
danced for joy before God
with all their might to the sound of singing,
of lyres, lutes, tambourines, cymbals and trumpets.
—1 Chronicles 13:8

For most Christians, it is safe to say, relationship to Christ does not determine their basic choices. Faith commitment is seldom the deciding factor in what kind of jobs people seek, or the place and type of homes in which they live, or even what lifestyle they choose. More often, perhaps, it may influence the choice of a husband or wife, or friends. But for the majority, these basic choices are first made, then baptized by bringing Jesus in after the fact to hallow the decisions that would have been made anyway. Jesus becomes an afterthought.

To a large extent this is because little connection is seen between liturgy and life. What is celebrated in church does not speak to the everyday reality that characterizes human life today. In church we deal with the realm of the holy. When we leave church we get back to reality. If our prayer has given us a bit more strength to live each day, we are grateful. But there is seldom the expectation that the liturgy will give us a vision or deeper appreciation of how to live our lives more meaningfully or purposefully.

What is there in the Sunday liturgy that could support us in our home lives? What are the connections between our faith as expressed in the liturgy and our work in the marketplace? These questions can never be answered if we think of the Sunday eucharist in the personal terms to which our consumer society has accustomed us. If the church primarily provides services to satisfy our personal needs, we will find it hard to understand that its real purpose is to submit us to the direction of God, allowing us to follow him, so that the dance may go on.

The church's liturgy, with its many moods and rhythms, leads us on life's journey in ways quite different from where the self-fulfillment gurus would take us. For it immerses us in the mystery of life where meaning and salvation is found in one who was nailed to a cross in an act of total self-giving.

Our renewed liturgy was meant to bring about the renewal of Christian life, said the Vatican Council. As the embodiment and summary of the riches of our faith, liturgy has the power to take our everyday lives and transform them, divinize them by bringing them into contact with the saving actions of Christ. But not if we persist in seeing it as a holy action quite apart from what life is all about.

Back in the early sixties, when I was in seminary, we were quite concerned about an incident that had taken place about a decade before in Canada. A priest who had publicly left the church and repudiated his priesthood was standing on a street corner when a bakery truck rolled to a stop. Extending his hand, he uttered, *"Hoc est enim Corpus meum"*—the words of consecration.

This threw the diocese into a theological panic. After all, he was a priest forever according to the order of Melchizedek. It was real bread in the truck. He said the right words. Was it or wasn't it now the body of Christ? Opinion was divided. To be safe, the bread was bought and given to an orphanage of young children so that there would not be any sacrilege. Just in case. . . .

Today we may laugh at a story like this. But it does serve to illustrate how easy it is to reduce liturgy to quasi-magic words and formulas quite divorced from the living reality in which they are embedded and which gives them their power. There is nothing magic or automatic about the eucharist. To have any meaning, it must be an expression of our lives, lives in which we accept the reality that God is the transcendental context in which we live and breathe and have our being.

From the perspective of the gathering rhythm, we might ask whether it is possible to celebrate the sacrament of community if there is not a celebrating community to speak of. Many people are uneasy when they find themselves in churches in which no one seems to take any interest in whether they are there or not. It seems a sort of countersign of what Christian life should be.

What needs to be asserted is that the community dimension or rhythm of eucharist requires that we make a conscious effort truly to live the fellowship that we celebrate. Our Christianity must begin to shape our self-understanding. The central Christian ethic of love hinges on a proper appreciation of the true nature of Christian community.

This is admittedly a difficult proposition, especially in modern society. A good deal of the imagery dealing with community may seem totally foreign to us. Yearning after community may appear to be nostalgia for some golden age, when things were simpler—perhaps. The fact remains: we need to translate the idea behind the gathering rhythm into understandable terms.

Our parishes today, more often than not, are large anonymous bodies reflecting somewhat the anonymity and tendency toward bureaucracy of society. We may not know more than a handful of people by name. Parish boundaries are blurred, and few people feel strong allegiance to "their" parish. And the entrance rite may give us no sense of belonging to a real family that is larger than our natural families.

However, it would be odd if the assembly did not develop any relations among those gathered. In the earliest days of the church, when Christians were outnumbered by their fellow Jews or pagans, it surely did so. Perhaps we need a conversion of outlook enabling us to see our Christian identity as a public responsibility to the larger society to which we belong. That seems to be what the early church tried to do within the Roman empire.

In two articles, "Eucharist" and "Community," which appeared in *Worship* almost two decades ago, Jerome Murphy-O'Connor gave a detailed study of community in the thought of St. Paul. He showed the depth and the realism of Paul's thought. It is the community that mediates the salvation won by Christ. The word that he spoke is not heard in the contemporary world unless it is proclaimed by the community, which becomes the incarnational prolongation of the mission of the saving Christ.

Murphy-O'Connor also makes the important point that Paul sees Jesus as the embodiment of authentic humanity. Christ is what all human beings were intended to be like from the beginning, a reality spoiled by sin. Unlike the vice lists of his contemporaries, when Paul lists the main sins of humankind (he has forty-four of them!), the vast majority are antisocial. He was convinced that sin reigns by dividing the world into isolated units where relationships are founded chiefly on self-interest.

In chapter 10, when Paul speaks of participation in the eucharist, he reminds us, "The cup of blessing that we bless, is it not a participation in the blood of Christ? The bread that we break, is it not a participation in the body of Christ?" (1 Cor 10:16). The word that is here translated by "participation" is *koinonia*, a key New Testament concept. We find it, for example, in the summary statements in Acts of what the Christian community was supposed to be.

Acts 4:32 (see also 2:42ff.) tells us that "the community of believers was of one heart and mind, and no one claimed that any of his possessions was his own, but they had everything in common." No hint of religious individualism here. They also tended to call themselves the "*ekklesia* of God," a phrase we now translate "church." This shows an extraordinary self-consciousness, whereby they accepted a responsibility for mediating to the world the saving power of Christ Jesus.

This was done concretely in a number of ways. Perhaps the most obvious was the elimination of social barriers. St. Paul was able to remind the Galatians that because of their baptism they were no longer Jew nor Greek, male nor female, slave nor free. The new relationships that were theirs excluded all discrimination and division. To a large extent, the early church was a classless society.

One of the most striking things about the Christian community in the first centuries was its ability to dissolve social and economic distinctions. The ethnic differences that separate people, the personal histories, which are often so disparate, all of these things set us up in different classes in the world in which we live. The eucharist demands that we meld people together into the one body of Christ, no matter what might otherwise seem to divide. The fact that people from every walk of life could gather around a common table was unheard of in ancient times. Doing so led admiring pagans to say of the fledgling Christian communities, "See how they love one another!"

Contemporary people seldom thought of the church in this way prior to the Second Vatican Council. We tended to think of the church as a perfect society, where the main emphasis was on its structural and institutional aspects. Thankfully, this element was downgraded at that council, which held out so many new possibilities that there is no longer any one dominant model that holds sway. Surely the most eucharistic model, however, is that of a community of disciples. When gathered around the Lord's table, people can reaffirm their common identity and recommit themselves to helping build the kingdom for which Jesus lived and died.

Baptism here gives us our primary identity. Being Christian is not the same thing as belonging to some sort of salvation club. Rather, being brought into God's family is like assuming a different nationality, with new and challenging relationships with all one's other sisters and brothers in Christ. In this sense Christianity is not simply something tacked on to one's being American, or Filipino, or anything else. It is what identifies someone as the person that he or she is. Personhood, in the Christian sense, is essentially relational.

Vatican II reintroduced us to the idea of our being a pilgrim people. At the very least this implies that we have not yet reached our final goal or destiny. We are still on the way, unfinished. But we are on the road together. We need not look for perfection in all of our companions. Our community is not a place where problems, imperfection, and sin are an exception. They are the rule. I like the answer one priest gave to the person who explained that he didn't go to church because it was full of hypocrites. "That's all right," the priest said. "There is always room for one more."

In our pluralistic age we cannot expect the liturgy's gathering rhythm to give us a sense of identity with the whole of our society. It can (and should) at least bond us more closely to our worshiping community. It can also serve to help us know ourselves as persons. The force of the ritual comes to bear on us individually, as the personal agents we should be as sisters or brothers of Christ.

How does this find practical application in everyday life? The first thing required is a new examination of conscience. Begin by throwing out the ten commandments—not their observance, just the idea that they sum up all of Christian life. I've always been amazed that we never learned to use the beatitudes, or the judgment scene in Matthew 25:31-46, or even the one commandment that Jesus gave us (Jn 13:34-35) as the gauge of true Christian action. To develop a liturgical spirituality, however, as this book tries to advance, we might use the rhythms of the eucharist.

What does it mean to be attentive to the gathering rhythm? It means recognizing that lack of unity and community are not from God and can never lead us back to the heart of our creator. This implies developing a concern for one another as well as for the poor and the oppressed. This is something that necessarily can be expressed in many ways. What we are speaking of is the ability to break down whatever it is that alienates people one from another, that breaks down community or fellowship.

Many do this already on the level of family. Efforts are also made to heal wounds, to reach out to the sick, to build bridges, to be peacemakers. None of this comes easily. The first thing it requires is a genuine compassion. We have to become other-oriented, allowing their need and pain to touch our hearts. Otherwise we won't even notice when others are bleeding. Even harder, it also requires that we learn to forgive.

Forgiveness is especially difficult for many, but it is one of the things Jesus told us in no uncertain terms that we should do. We are to forgive seven times seventy times (Mt 18:22). We are even to love our enemies and do good to those who hate us (Mt 5:44). In the Our Father we pray that we be forgiven as we have forgiven others. And we are to do this with such sincerity that we can, like Jesus, pray that God forgive them also because "they know not what they do" (Lk 23:34).

A vision of this sort comes only from faith. It is easy to remain on the surface, seeing only our own hurt. We are quick to observe the sins of others. It takes little skill to notice another's weaknesses or defects. We all have them. But to look deeper and see the spark of the divine that God has placed in each one, to recognize Christ in the broken members of his body comes from a knowledge that only a loving faith can provide.

What we are dealing with here is the effort to make situations and people whole. It means learning to build up rather than to tear down. There are many opportunities do to this on a daily basis, whether at home or among people with whom we work or socialize. All it requires is a sensitivity to ways of spreading Christ's love, rather than thinking that we have been good little Christians as long as we succeed in "avoiding sin."

Then there is the larger question of our responsibility for making this a world of reconciliation and peace. We need a deeper awareness of the many ways in which we collude in the exploitation of others by our silence or our complicity. Sin used to be easy enough to figure out when it was personal and dealt with simple things like stealing, murder, or adultery. But now there is a realization that sin can go beyond individuals and become embedded in the very structures of the world in which we live.

These social sins are new to us. It is only recently that we began hearing about the sins of sexism, racism, and various forms of prejudice. We are just beginning to face questions like how Americans—being only a minority of the world's population—can justify using more than half of the world's resources. Is it sufficient to say that we do nothing personally to hurt or oppress others, or has the time come to do something positive to eliminate some of these evils?

We can easily become cynical and say that there is nothing that can be done. But there are countless examples of people who have made a real difference in the world because of their concern. It could be by church, school, or political involvement at various levels. Even writing letters to our officials, letting them know of our convictions and concerns would be better than nothing.

Surely parishes might become communities where the needs of members can be taken care of from the resources of the parish itself. There is no reason why only the priests should be expected to visit the sick, attend the wakes, welcome newcomers into the parish, counsel the troubled, conduct Bible study, give relief to the poor, visit the hospitals and nursing homes regularly, bring communion to shut-ins, and do whatever else needs to be done.

A parish should be a sort of organic unit whereby the people are related to one another through participation in a common life. By sharing the responsibilities of mutual care and concern, they help each other become free to be what God wants us all to be—liberated from the self-centeredness that provokes sin and strife. A group that has truly put on "the mind of Christ" (1 Cor 2:16) and addressed itself to the betterment of its communities gives powerful witness to the power of the Holy Spirit in our midst.

If there is one thing that characterized Jesus' ministry, it was that his concern for others was expressed in an outreach to those who were lost. Unlike other rabbis, he did not simply set up shop and wait for people to come to him. Rather, he saw it as his responsibility to reach out to "the lost sheep of the house of Israel" (Mt 10:6). Can members of his body do any less?

In many third-world countries, the church has taken a "preferential option for the poor." This has been criticized by those who feel that it is not the task of the church to get involved in the public arena. There is a strain of pietist Christianity that strives only to put individuals in correct relationship with God with little concern to put them into proper relationships with one another. Church forays into the social justice field are derided and called Marxist, accused of having no connection with the gospel. Again, Dom Helder Camara had an answer: "When I feed the poor, everyone calls me a saint. But when I ask why the poor are hungry, everyone calls me a communist."

Our concern for the poor is not only because Jesus was born poor, but because in his own ministry the poor were those with whom he most closely identified. Jesus was constantly criticized by the Pharisees for his outreach to the marginalized of society and those they considered beyond the law. Jesus reached out to them not out of pity but out of love. They were his sisters and brothers.

An ancient rabbi once asked his disciples, "When is it light enough to see?" "I know," one answered. "It is light enough to see when I can distinguish an oak from a maple." "No," said the rabbi. "I know," a second volunteered. "It is light enough to see when I can tell a horse from a cow." "That is not correct either," noted the rabbi. There being no other attempts at an answer, the rabbi stated, "It is light enough to see when I can look a person in the face and recognize a brother or sister."

4

The Storytelling Rhythm

I danced on a Friday
when the sun turned black—
It's hard to dance
with the devil on your back.
They buried my body
and they thought I'd gone—
But I am the dance
and I still go on.

Once the community has gathered, it is time to tell the stories. For it is the word of God that calls us together and accompanies us as a lamp for our steps. We are a "people of the book," and our faith is embodied in the scriptures. It is a faith that has roots thousands of years old, and it rests in the conviction that God has chosen us as his people.

The biblical revelation we are able to share at mass goes beyond the history of God's dealing with a people. It is primarily revelation about a person. As the beginning of the letter to the Hebrews puts it, "In times past, God spoke in partial and various ways to our ancestors through the prophets; in these last days, he spoke to us through a son" (Heb 1:1-2). We gather to immerse ourselves in and be formed by Christ's story.

Robert Bellah, in *Habits of the Heart*, notes that communities, in a sense, are constituted by their past.

In order not to forget that past, he adds, a community must be involved in retelling its story, its constitutive narrative. In so doing it holds up examples of the men and women who have embodied and exemplified the meaning of the community. These stories of collective history and exemplary individuals are an important part of the tradition which is central to any community.

Obviously, the stories of the Christian community go beyond those of a tribe, country, or any other group. Our stories are mainly those enshrined in the Bible. And we know biblical narratives to have been inspired by God. We have the Jewish Bible (the Old Testament), since Jesus never repudiated the history of salvation contained therein. It was the Jewish scriptures that helped Jesus form his own understanding of the God of salvation. For us, of course, more emphasis is placed on the New Testament, seen as the full flowering of Old Testament revelation and as the story of Jesus himself.

The New Testament is especially important because it enshrines the heart of the Christian myth. *Myth* does not imply a fairytale. The term is an important one, however, because it dramatizes the fact that some stories are more central to the self-understanding of the group than others. Precisely because of that importance, they become pivotal to the group and are determinative of its life.

Every religious group has a key myth, which underlies its theology and practice, its worship and way of life. The central myth of the later Jewish Bible, for example, is the Mosaic covenant. The other biblical narratives are told in relation to this key incident, which serves to give meaning to the rest of the Old Testament.

Likewise for Christians. The story of Christ's death, resurrection, and ascension is the core myth on which everything else rests. St. Paul reminds his Corinthians of this by saying, "I handed on to you as of first importance what I also received: that Christ died for our sins in accordance with the scriptures; that he was buried; that he was raised on the third day in accordance with the scriptures" (1 Cor 15:3-4).

Giving mythological value to the death/resurrection/ascension of Christ does not rob the myth of its historical reality. On the contrary, the fact that we can claim historical validity for our myth renders it even more immediate to our daily experience. For, as Robert Bellah again points out, the memories that tie us to the past also turn us toward the future as communities of hope. They carry, he says, "a context of meaning that can allow us to connect our aspirations for ourselves and those closest to us with the aspirations of a larger whole and see our own efforts as being, in part, contributions to the common good."

Focusing on the death/resurrection/ascension does not lessen the value of the rest of the scriptures. Everything in the scriptures helps us to appreciate more fully the core myth, which gives focus to it all. It is important to understand more fully the varied values that surround and enrich our myth. We always have the need to appreciate more and more what it means to us as members of the same religious community. This is good news!

If we spoke of the redemption as involving only Jesus' sufferings and death it would not be a very inspiring story. The first Christians were so discouraged by this that some of them decided to quit the Christian community and go back home. There they could pick up the scattered pieces of their lives. The thought of "what happened in Jerusalem these past few days" filled them only with a despondency sapping all hope. For them, it was bad news.

It would have remained bad news had there been no resurrection. It would also have been a tragedy if Jesus had been killed by falling off a roof, or hit by some runaway horse. Jesus' death, however, was not accidental. It came as a result of choices and risks that he took. Refusing to abandon the will of the Father, it became the price of fidelity to his mission and calling.

His death also came as the culmination of a life of service. Throughout the gospels we see Jesus arousing the ire of the scribes and Pharisees by reaching out to "the lost sheep of the house of Israel." He was constantly accused of eating and drinking with sinners and tax collectors. It was because Jesus was concerned about the poor and the oppressed that he did this, and that he was willing to die. Greater love than this no one has. This is good news for us.

Saying that this is our central myth means that it is meant to be the pattern of all Christian life. Those of us who claim that we have been touched by Christ need to have like attitudes, commitments, and choices. And we can choose them because we have come to know that doing so brings life. This yields us a vision of a people gathered to be fed by Christ. This is important because, if we ever lose the sense of our core myth, our ritual becomes sheer magic.

We mentioned in the previous chapter the incident of an ex-priest saying the words of consecration over a bakery truck and the theological questions that this raised. One of the things that could have been said about this is that there was obviously no proclamation of the word of God on that occasion. Consequently, there was no real intention of situating those words within the myth that undergirds our ritual. Lacking this, to think that the mere words could bring about Christ's eucharistic presence is to give independent value to empty sounds. As sure as anything, this reduces the liturgy to magic. It would be no more than hocus pocus.

This fact alone helps us to appreciate the place of the word of God in the celebration of the liturgy. It prevents the ritual from taking on an independent life of its own. It is also a manifestation of the power of God's word. Psychologically and theologically, it is as we read in the incident of the two disciples on the road to Emmaus. They were able to recognize the risen Lord in the breaking of the bread only after their hearts were set on fire by the discussion of the scriptures that took place before it.

In this case, the proclamation of the scriptures was an enabling reality. It still serves to open the mind, thus helping us to become both communities of memory and of hope in today's world. On life's road, searching for meaning, we are able to find it in the breaking of the bread, where we recognize that true life can be found only when life is given for others.

And so, as soon as the community has gathered, we once again retell the story of salvation. And if the assembly itself is a manifestation of Christ's presence, he is also revealed in a very real way in the proclamation of the scriptures. It is a presence we have too long ignored.

Since the Vatican Council, we have begun to think of the mass as being divided into two main parts: the liturgy of the word, and the liturgy of the eucharist. Both are essential to the eucharistic celebration. This statement might seem self-evident, but it was not always so. For centuries we have neglected giving the scriptures the importance they deserve. From the time of the Reformation, because Protestants stressed the word, we stressed the sacrament. Both of us have been impoverished as a result.

Before Vatican II we used to speak of the "important parts" of the mass. For the legal minded, this meant that one could not miss any of these without serious sin. The liturgy of the word was not included among these important parts. Now it must be admitted that the way some liturgies of the word are celebrated it doesn't seem that it would be much of a sin to miss them. Nevertheless, this section of the mass is as important as the liturgy of the eucharist.

In order to help us appreciate the scriptures more, the renewal of the liturgy that took place after the Vatican Council decided on using three readings rather than two. It also utilized a three-year cycle rather than the yearly recurrent plan that was in vogue up till then. The whole purpose of this was to expose God's community to a richer scriptural fare. To drive home the meaning of the scriptures for us today, the homily was also mandated at all community celebrations.

Sadly, it is only since the Vatican Council that we find canon law requiring a homily at all Sunday liturgies. Before that they were simply recommended. The church now recognizes that the proclamation of the word requires explanation in order to explicate its meaning for us today. The homily—which differs from a sermon—is not a learned exposition about what the scriptures meant when they were written. Rather, it tries to face the community with what they mean to us *now*, wherever we happen to be. If Jesus is to be found in the proclamation, he is there only in the present tense.

Unwilling to carry its logic to its ultimate conclusions when it came to daily homilies, however, the code only recommended them. What all this shows is that at the practical level we still do not place overmuch importance on preaching. To the extent that we continue to diminish the homily, however, we impoverish our liturgy. The word of God is not truly proclaimed unless it becomes actual again today.

The liturgy of the word, in a sense, is a dialogue between God and us. Everything builds up to and leads to the gospel reading. With the three-year cycle we have at present, this gives us a chance to focus on the portrait of Jesus sketched by each of the synoptic writers in turn, as we spend a year each on Matthew, Mark, and Luke. The readings are more or less continuous, taking in the entirety of Jesus' public life during the Sundays of Ordinary Time.

First, however, we hear a reading from the Old Testament. This is always chosen in relation to the gospel. There is more trouble with the second reading, from the New Testament, which runs on a semi-continuous track of its own, often seeming to have little to do with the general gospel theme. It needs to be accepted for what it is, and as a sort of side fare for our edification and for reflection during the week.

After the readings there is time for a bit of silent reflection. This is where we can begin to discern what God is saying to us that day. These rare silences should be treasured and not allowed to become a general distraction period. Also, the first reading is always followed by a responsorial psalm to help focus our response to God's word. God speaks; we respond.

The alleluia that precedes the gospel, and the candles and incense that sometimes accompany its reading, serve to remind us that the aim of the gospel goes beyond pouring more information into our heads. Space is made for the senses and for the heart, that we might be moved by the unutterable groans of the Spirit.

It is the homily, of course, that attempts to tie the entire liturgy of the word together for the assembly. It is the function of the homily to make Jesus present to the faith-consciousness of the community. And just as the liturgy itself takes in all moments of time—it is praise of God for the wonders of creation, thanksgiving for the work of redemption in Christ, and a prayer for the Holy Spirit to transform us into the body of Christ—so also does the homily deal with the past, present, and future.

The gospels speak of Jesus' past deeds. But we listen to them aware of the fact that somehow his story is bound up with our own, here and now. We remain the continuing objects of his love and concern. Challenged to incarnate once again his attitudes, ideals, his sense of mission and calling, Jesus becomes intensely present to our minds and hearts. He is no longer a distant memory, because we know that his saving actions of the past are still effective in the present.

Furthermore, we are gathered together at a meal where Christ himself is the host. We share at his table as members of his family. In this sense, as risen Lord, Jesus is part of God's larger plan for creation, a plan that is still unfolding. It is Jesus who gives meaning to this plan as well as to our participation in it. It is only in Christ that we are being saved even as we listen.

The homily also looks to the future—our awareness that the kingdom has still not arrived, and that all of creation still groans until the fullness of the redemption is manifested. The eucharistic assembly itself is a microcosm of the heavenly banquet. As we sing each week after the words of institution, Christ will come again. This assurance is a gift of the Spirit, a pledge of future glory.

The main nagging problem that remains is that many eucharists do not bring us face to face with Christ in this way. Few celebrations give us a sense of communication with our risen Lord. What can be done to make the telling of our story more compelling?

Martin Buber tells an oft-repeated tale involving his own grandfather, who was paralyzed. As a Hasidic Jew, he had a great admiration for the founder of the movement, Baal Shem Tov. Now Baal Shem Tov had a rather ecstatic manner of prayer, in which he would dance and jump in transports of joy. One day someone was asking the grandfather to describe how this was done. As his memory became more and more vivid, the old man became increasingly animated. Soon he was out of his wheelchair demonstrating what he was talking about. He was cured.

That's how a good story should be told.

I once had a marvelous lector in my parish. Possessed of a rich baritone voice, he was also a trained speaker, a speech professor at the university. It was always a joy to hear him read. I mentioned to him once that, much as I liked his reading, it seemed to me that he always did a better job on the second reading.

He smiled sheepishly and said, "Maybe that's because I like St. Paul." It turned out that he not only liked Paul, he had a complete set of commentaries on the Pauline letters. He never got up to proclaim the scriptures without first reading the commentary and praying over the readings. It showed. He was giving us Paul from the inside.

I might add that I was not one of those democratically minded pastors who believed in giving everyone with good will a chance to be lector. Lectors are ministers of the word to the community. Their choice should come from their having a charism for communication. Choosing anyone, good or bad, prepared or unprepared, trivializes God's word. It is equally difficult to come out with a convincing "The word of the Lord!" when we have read from a sheet of paper or from a missalette.

Aside from these seemingly obvious minutiae, John Shea has tried to isolate three characteristics of effective storytelling for us. The first is very simply the telling and retelling of the stories. This is never boring. We need only consider the experience we have all had of children's delight in having their favorite stories read to them over and over again. If anyone dares to leave out a page or to change a section, they are quick to accuse you of having changed the story. For them that is always unacceptable. Good stories need to be retold often. The more often the better.

That is why what we remember most about the gospels are Jesus' stories. People are familiar with the story of the prodigal son (or father!), the good Samaritan, and other stories, even though they may be unfamiliar with much of the other teaching that the gospels contain. It's hard to forget a good story.

Second, the very retelling forms pervasive attitudes and outlooks on life's mystery in the community. Good stories are always open to deeper interpretation. They touch us at the core of our being. The more often we hear them, the more meaning they seem to have. They strike us in new and varied ways.

Finally, in addition to enabling reflection on life's mystery and to forming enduring convictions and attitudes, good storytelling engenders a certain moral sensitivity to gospel values. This often precipitates a moral struggle as we examine our lives against the ideals pictured in the story, or as we pit the values of the story against the values of the society in which we live. This will be dealt with more fully when we take up the prophetic rhythm.

Thus the liturgy requires that God's word not only be proclaimed, but that those who gather become personally involved in and with it. How is this done? It seems to me that there are several necessary steps.

In the first place, there must be the realization that Jesus is revealed to us in the proclamation of the scriptures. Unless we have some expectation and conviction in this regard, we can view the liturgy of the word as being just a (sometimes boring) preliminary ritual before the real thing—reception of communion. The scriptures must be taken seriously. They can reveal Jesus to us.

Then, we must listen to the scriptures actively. In other words, we must let our own story be challenged by them. We look for the message there is for us in the various readings. We begin to question the readings, to connect them with other scripture passages, to sense their actuality today. The Bible brings a message of life and hope for people in a particular time and place. The scriptures challenge particular communities to be faithful, each in their own way.

Finally, we must each take personal responsibility for the story. Ultimately, the scriptures touch us as individuals within the community. We can only add to the dynamism of the Christian community to which we belong when we begin to take the gospel seriously.

This is something that we can do whether or not we are happy with the proclamation of the scriptures in our church. There is no need to moan and groan if the homily seems out of place or ill prepared. If we have prepared the readings before the liturgy, we will be in a position to wrestle personally with the readings, asking how they challenge us in a particular way. How would we preach these same readings? Why? Asking questions like this can make the difference between frustration and meaningful participation.

The storytelling rhythm is one of total immersion in the Christ event. It is being able to see Christ's life, death, and resurrection as good news. For the tomb did not hold Christ for long, and the dance that is still his can also be ours.

5

With Open Minds: Abiding in the Truth

And all shall sing, in their festive dance:
"My home is within you."
—*Psalm 87:7*

Insisting that we must be a community that is formed by the word of God may strike some as a bit strange. The scriptures seem such an obvious part of Christianity. However, until recently, Catholic piety has been nourished more by the sacraments and devotions of various kinds: novenas, the rosary, personal prayer, and so forth. For the last thousand years we were not overmuch given to the scriptures. Even in the twentieth century one couldn't automatically assume that every Catholic home had a Bible. Until the Second Vatican Council, at least, it was regarded almost as a Protestant book. Because of our fear of the possible excesses of private interpretation, we tended to leave these things to the clergy, and to believe and behave as we were told.

Suddenly, we are told that our faith and piety must be based on the word of God. Every sacramental rite has been revised to include a liturgy of the word. There are numerous choices for the various readings and the possibility of choosing others that seem more appropriate. Though this may be nothing new theologically, from a practical point of view it represents a polar shift.

Now we hear from the council and from the pope not only that the scriptures are important, but that in their proclamation we have a real presence of Christ. Though different, it is a presence just as real as the eucharistic presence. When the two disciples on the road to Emmaus exclaimed, "Were not our hearts burning within us as he spoke to us on the way and opened the scriptures to us?" (Lk 24:32) the implication is that had this not taken place, ultimately they would not have been able to recognize Jesus in the breaking of the bread. We cannot limit the ways in which God is revealed to us without impoverishing our ability to recognize God at all.

If we return to the story of the Emmaus disciples, we can discover there a familiar pattern. The story begins as most real stories do—with people struggling to make sense out of life. The starting point deals with one of life's "why" questions. Clear answers are hard to come by with questions such as these, despite the fact that we so often have to wrestle with the mystery of suffering and death, or of the seeming triumph of evil.

Why is a young child suddenly stuck down in the prime of life by some crippling disease? Why did a loved parent have to suffer for years, wasting away before eventually succumbing to death? Why are some deprived of the means of being able to care for their families because of impersonal management decisions? Why does God allow evil and sin to reign with such seeming impunity? Why? It is life's "why" questions that give purpose and direction to life itself.

The problem the two disciples on life's road were trying to resolve illustrates this. Why did Jesus have to suffer and die just when it seemed that his kingdom was about to be established? Why were his enemies able to ride so roughshod over him? What was the meaning of their own lives now that the source of their hope had gone from them? Again, why?

At the beginning of their journey they could come up with no good answers to these questions. So they were giving up. In quitting the Christian community in Jerusalem, they had really decided that it was impossible to make sense out of anything that had happened. So discouraged were they that they did not even recognize the one whom they were mourning when he joined them on their journey.

So Jesus tried to turn them to deeper reflection. Note that their reflections were done in common. Life is easier to fathom and to manage when we can share our concerns and questions with others who have had similar experiences. When life has been shattered, we require a new life synthesis. Hence the need for reflection. For Christians, the scriptures provide the key for these reflections. So Jesus guided them in trying to understand what had happened by "opening the scriptures" to them.

This led them not only to integrate their understanding of what had happened, at the same time acquiring a deeper and better understanding of the reality of their lives, but it enabled them also to *act* as Christians. When they reached Emmaus, they did not turn in on themselves once again in self-pity. Instead, they invited the stranger in to share their hospitality. The exercise of charity ever remains at the heart of the gospel, defining what Christianity is all about. St. John is able to summarize everything Jesus wanted us to do with the simple injunction, "As I have loved you, so you also should love one another" (Jn 13:34).

The final stage of the process came with their ability to recognize Jesus in the breaking of the bread. This discovery enabled them to return to Jerusalem to pick up their lives where they had left off. Having been tempted to abandon their Christian vocation, they find themselves once more in the company of disciples.

We might note that this is a recurring process. We are constantly called to reintegrate our understanding of life. Jerusalem was not the end of the Emmaus story. As they told the disciples there what had happened to them on life's road, they also heard the stories of those who had remained behind. The ability to reflect further on this led them to leave Jerusalem to bring the good news "to all the nations" (Lk 24:47). That was yet another story, one filled with experiences that would again test their faith and determination, thus providing still more material for thought and reflection.

If we are truly part of a community of living memory, our life's synthesis must be based on the experience and wisdom of the group. On Sundays we gather for a ritualization of the life and teaching of Christ, who provides the basis of that memory. His message, however, must be reflected on and carried out in our daily lives. Otherwise it will not permeate our understanding and practice. If our integrating principle comes from Confucius, Zen, or the current pop guru, we can hardly lay claim to be Christian. It does make a difference.

Years ago, I faced the necessity of telling my father that his sickness (cancer) was terminal. It was around 5:00 A.M., and the rest of the family was still asleep. Both early risers, we used these quiet hours to solve the problems of the world. Now, the focus was closer to home. As we sipped our coffee, we were wrestling with the mystery of our own life and death. Deep down I sensed that Dad already knew. It was the Sunday after Easter.

Later that day we celebrated mass with our family and cousins who had come to visit. As we discussed the scriptures, everyone seemed to be very circumspect, tiptoeing gingerly around the fact of Dad's impending death. Finally, Dad himself said, "I suppose you are all waiting for me to say something." What he shared was simply the consolation he felt by reason of his belief in the resurrection, which meant that his death was only a door to a new and better life where some day we could all be rejoined. Sharing the same faith and accepting the scriptures we had just read about Jesus' own triumph over death helped us to see Dad's death as something that was part of all of us, that we could talk about or cry over together. Most important, we could support one another with the hope that came from the mystery of Christ, which we lived and breathed. I have been much more comfortable with the thought of my own death since that time.

The Sunday liturgy attempts to give us a basic foundation for our Christian memory. Though it tries to do so by going through all four gospels in more or less systematic fashion, this is hardly sufficient. If our only familiarity with the scriptures is what we hear in church, we are living on a starvation diet. Ours must be lives that are based solidly on biblical revelation.

Having a biblical spirituality means that we must be at least as familiar with the scriptures as we are with the workings of the stock market or world events. Most of us can spend hours devouring newspapers or watching TV news, while leaving the Bible to gather dust on the shelf. It is admired from a distance, revered from afar. Instead, it must be a favorite book to which we return time and again for the pure pleasure that it affords.

There are several reasons for this. One is linked with the celebration of mass itself. People often complain that the liturgy is boring, or that the scriptures are next to meaningless. Admittedly, not all presiders are able to make the readings come to life. But not even the best of them should be expected to do all the work. It is impossible for them to do so.

In order to profit from the Sunday liturgies, it is important that we not go there "cold." If we have no idea what the readings will be until we hear them (what an act of faith in the lectors or the PA system!) we are giving less thought to what we are about than we give to selecting the clothes we will wear. How can we carry on a mental dialogue with the readings or with the homily if all we have to rely on is first impressions?

Preparing for the Sunday liturgy is a two-pronged task. The most immediate is to prepare and then reflect upon the readings for each week. This requires little more than reading them a day or so before, in order to begin thinking about their meaning and how they relate to our lives. A habit like this enables the scriptures to work their way into our subconscious, penetrating more and more deeply into our hearts. This, combined with a follow-up after the mass, enables us to embed the meaning even more deeply into our minds. Preparatory reading is only half the battle, however. It is critical to ponder the Sunday readings the following week as well. That way, guided (hopefully) by the homily, we can apply their message concretely to our lives, allowing them to sink deeper roots into our consciousness.

The second aspect of being ready for our Sunday celebrations might be termed remote preparation. This means simply the ability to be so familiar and comfortable with the scriptures that they become "our" book. While this process of familiarization might seem remote to any specific liturgy, it is surely not remote from what should be a continuing effort to center our lives more and more on the values that are enshrined in the scriptures.

In regard to the liturgy, there is an importance in knowing the background and context of the Bible stories that we hear week after week. The Sunday scripture passages are wrenched out of context. All we hear is a snippet from this or that gospel, often in abbreviated form. Many of the Old Testament passages are strangely unfamiliar. To the extent that we can reintegrate these into their living context in the life of our faith community, we will be able to see the Bible as a living whole, which gradually reveals itself to us. It will enable us to realize, as the psalmist says, that the source of all good is truly in God.

Admittedly, today most of us labor under a disadvantage. The Bible is no longer the common possession or treasure of the entire Christian community. Years ago biblical stories provided the inspiration for much of our literature. It could be assumed that people would be familiar with the Old as well as the New Testament. Now we find ourselves in a position where the homilist has to explain what the readings are all about before he can get down to the task of trying to apply them to our lives.

To the extent that this is true, we have remedial work to do. The scriptures testify to God's ever-active and effective will to save us throughout human history.

The more familiar we become with the Bible, the more we can see its interrelatedness. The New Testament writers presumed a familiarity with the scriptures in their hearers. There are so many allusive references to the Old Testament in the New that we really cannot expect to understand it fully unless we view the entire Bible as a whole.

As God's own self-revelation, the Bible should form the natural basis of our prayer. Books may be helpful, but they can never replace the word of God. If our personal lives and spirituality are not based on the Bible, we run the danger of losing our story. Instead of knowing where our treasure lies, we become eclectic; we seek here and there for nourishment without having any solid foundation on which to rely and against which to test whatever comes our way.

There are several ways of making the scriptures central to our spirituality. The first is simply familiarizing ourselves with them. They should be part of our weekly, if not daily reading. It would be helpful to have a plan to read the entire Bible in the course of a year. This would require only four chapters a day, even allowing for a few lapses here and there.

Second, we should incorporate some study into our reading. Many Bibles have substantial notes to help us better understand the text or to acquaint us with variant readings. They also have introductions to the major sections of the Bible and to individual books. This allows us to read with more sophistication, aware of the type of literature that we are dealing with, the time of its composition, its authorship, and other important background.

We can no longer afford to be as naive as we were in the past. It helps to know that St. Paul did not write the Letter to the Hebrews, or that the gospel writers were not necessarily eyewitnesses to the events they describe. It makes a difference if Mark was written before the other gospels, just as it does if Moses did not write the entire Pentateuch.

We can progress beyond the notes by using a commentary on individual books. There are various kinds. Some of the simpler ones attempt to help us understand better what the individual writers were trying to convey. It is not accidental that the synoptic gospels tell the same story in slightly different ways. These stories play varying roles in their gospels. Knowing the intention of the authors helps us to interpret them better, aware of how the one message of Christ is capable of being expressed in different ways and of being applied to different life situations.

Were we to concentrate even on one major book a year, in five years we would have been able to tackle the gospels and the Book of Acts. Another similar time frame could help us do the same with the Pauline epistles. As we progress is this way, we not only deepen understanding, we develop a greater confidence in our ability to dialogue with the text and discern the values enshrined there.

There is no reason why all this should be done alone. Today there are a variety of Bible study groups to help us deepen our appreciation of the text. Some are purely study groups; others are more prayer sessions. Whichever we prefer, it is always a salutary corrective to allow another's understanding to impinge on ours. It is all too easy to read with blinders on, blocking out some of the text's meaning. Others help keep us more radically honest in our effort to appreciate God's word, and how his community is guided by the wisdom of the Holy Spirit.

The process of gradual familiarization will inevitably influence our prayer. Indeed, scripture will form the basis of our prayer. In the early church the monks used to speak of "divine reading." By this they meant the prayerful reading of the word of God. It suffices to read a passage slowly, allowing whatever thoughts and prayers come to mind to be offered up to God. If a particular section seems more appropriate or meaningful, all we need do is pause a while and allow it to inspire whatever acts of gratitude or praise, or of sorrow and petition are appropriate.

Scriptural prayer is open to the inspiration of the Holy Spirit. After all, we hold that the Spirit was the inspiring force behind the entire Bible. To allow our prayer to be shaped by the faith-consciousness of generations of believers enables us to be guided gently by the hand of God. It helps direct our thoughts and actions into the ways of God's peace. It gives us the satisfaction of knowing that we are being open to the direction of our creator and redeemer.

In a very real sense, the Bible is God's own self-revelation and communication to us. If we believe that we are not the center of the universe, but that we have been loved into being by God, why is there so much reluctance to live by the book that comes from God? It would seem strange if we were to leave letters from a loved one unread. Yet, that is what we are doing when we make so little effort to come to appreciate God's mind and heart.

God's efforts at communication embrace different levels, just as our own human communication does. The letters we send when we are distanced from those we love are gratefully received. However, they lack the warmth and immediacy of personal presence. We might use friends to convey messages to family and loved ones back home. They, at least, would be able to communicate something more immediate because of their contact with us, wherever we might happen to be. Best of all, however, is the ability to return personally to visit and share our hopes and our love directly.

The Letter to the Hebrews begins by reminding us that God has tried all three of these methods in an effort to speak to our hearts. The scriptures record the faith struggle of a people attempting to come face to face with God. Besides this written word, however, we know that in former times God has spoken to us through his friends, the prophets. Despite their recognized closeness to God, they were not always well received. Finally, in our own time God has enfleshed himself, speaking to us through his Son, the one whom St. John can rightly call the Word-made-flesh.

In the case of Jesus, we are dealing with the living Word of God. The key to his power, to his ability to speak "with authority" comes from the fact that there was no discrepancy between what he said and who he was. The man was the message. It was not so much a question of Jesus practicing what he preached; rather, he preached what he himself practiced and lived. His person and message were one and the same. Jesus, as they used to say, had it all together.

The problem is that we seldom apply this lesson to ourselves. The passage where we are told that we should be able to do even greater works than Jesus is not taken seriously (cf. Jn 14:12). Neither is the one from John's prologue (Jn 1:13), where the assurance is found that all who accept Christ are—like him—enabled to become children of God, born not because of human passion or will, but from God. This sounds so suspiciously like the terminology used of the virgin birth that the first edition of the *Jerusalem Bible* used a convoluted variant enabling us to avoid the implications of the text.

The implications are simple: the disciple is expected to be like the master. We don't do all our scripture reading to make Bible experts of ourselves. We do it so that we can actually become manifestations of Christ and of Godlike living. By being open to the truth of God, we can ourselves become truth, become light and salt, and a word of salvation. The word of God in our own lives must become so much part of us that we can be identified with it. Only then will people come to see that it is a word of life.

6

The Prophetic Rhythm

I danced on the sabbath
And I cured the lame.
The holy people
Said it was a shame.
They whipped and they stripped
and they hung me high;
And they left me there
on a cross to die.

There is a story that is especially appropriate since we have been reappraising the impact of Columbus's discovery. It deals with Francisco Pizzaro, one of the conquistadors who helped secure the American continent for Spain. Best known for having conquered the Incan empire, Pizzaro knew his business. Audacious to a fault, he was willing to give the Incas a chance. He told Atahualpa, the ruler of the Incas, that he should submit to both the pope and the emperor.

The choices didn't please Atahualpa overmuch, and he replied that from what he knew of Christianity Christians believed in a God who had been killed by his own people. Since he felt his gods were alive and well, he could see no benefit in abandoning them. As for the emperor, while he was willing to extend brotherhood to Charles V, he saw no reason to pay him tribute. So the answer was no on that score as well.

Pizzaro and his men, having previously fortified themselves by confession as well as by mass and communion, then surprised Atahualpa and, with gun and cannon, proceeded to slaughter well over three thousand unarmed men, not to mention women and children.

Wasn't that a great mass!

This may be a particularly horrible example, but history affords many stories of how the eucharist has been used to justify very unchristian behavior. We may have been less blatant, but we can look back in shame on segregated churches and on slaveowners piously receiving communion before selling off women and children like so many cattle. We can detail how conquerors, oppressors, and exploiters of various stripes have gathered at the Lord's table.

If we are to turn to our own time, we can point to those who rape the land, engage in practices that threaten our entire banking system, keep people in economic peonage, and otherwise enrich themselves at the expense of others. Yet these same people see nothing anomalous about going to church and joining in the church's liturgy. Why?

The answer is simple: we have lost sight of the prophetic rhythm of eucharist. Reduced to a ritual that makes us feel good, it has been used mainly for our consolation. Jesus, however, did not give us the eucharist to make us feel good. He wanted it to enable us to *be* good. The eucharist is not a reward for the just; it is food for the journey.

There is a cutting edge to the gospel. We should approach it with fear and trembling, realizing that God's ways are not our ways (Is 55:8-9). A properly celebrated eucharist should bring about a cosmic change in our way of thinking and behaving. That's what it means to put on the mind of Christ Jesus (Phil 2:5).

Thus, an essential part of the liturgy of the word is its prophetic rhythm. God's word should challenge us to insert ourselves more deeply into God's own way of life—even if holy people think it is a shame. God's word, indeed the eucharist itself, is not there simply to fill us with security, but to stir us to help create the world God has wanted from the beginning of creation. It is the continuing task of disciples to be committed to the kingdom for which Jesus lived and died.

Before the Second Vatican Council, the eucharist was conceived as essentially a ritual performed by the priest. We had lost sight of the role of the community and saw the priest as a sacrificial personage, much after the model of the Old Testament priests. This sacrificial role was exercised especially during the eucharistic prayer, which, as proper to the priest, was said silently. Such a eucharist stressed the vertical relationship between God and creation, and the adoration owed to God on the part of his creatures.

In contrast to this emphasis on eucharist as eternal sacrifice, the days following the council began to see a greater emphasis placed on the horizontal dimension of the eucharist. In rediscovering the meal aspects of the liturgy, with the appropriate awareness of the interrelatedness of people gathered around a common table, the mass became a celebration and expression of fellowship.

Too exclusive a stress on the horizontal dimension, focused as it is on the human element, tends to give us a folksy eucharist. While this can be more appealing than the somewhat formal and austere liturgies of yesteryear, it can lead to too exclusive a focus on our own actions rather than those of Christ. This is as out of place as a liturgy where the vertical stress yields a God-and-me cultic celebration. A prophetic understanding of the eucharist, however, helps us to combine both aspects in a mutually reinforcing way.

The prophetic rhythm reminds us both of our dependence on God and our responsibilities to our neighbor. Each pole feeds the other. This can help us avoid the religious temptations of an individualistic or too humanistic piety, as well as the supernaturalism of a sacrificial ritualism. God wishes a worship that is expressed only when we "offer [our] bodies as a living sacrifice, holy and pleasing to God" (Rom 12:1).

Our worship "in the Spirit" is not a matter of special practices, but a matter of lifestyle. Nor is it a life we invent ourselves. It comes from God. Eucharist is thus not so much something we give to God, but something God gives to us in Christ. It must be received humbly in gratitude and adoration. It must also be responded to and reflected in our daily lives.

A prophetic liturgy helps us avoid the compartmentalization we tend to introduce into our religious practice. If we put God into the airtight container of the transcendent or the supernatural, our faith is sealed off from our daily life. When we see our ordinary relationships as both informed by and expressive of our faith and our worship, then we begin to integrate liturgy and life in a vital way. The liturgy provides the dynamic whereby we continue to grow in the same way that Jesus did.

The real story of the eucharist is that of a life given for others. We are constantly brought face to face with the self-giving of Christ, which becomes the model for us as well. As we are reminded in Jesus' prayer the night before he died "that we all may be one" (Jn 17:21), we cannot share at the Lord's table if we are alienated from any of the members of his body. This oneness is something that Jesus was willing to die for.

The prophetic element prevents us from settling into complacency and stagnation, from celebrating eucharists that cease to challenge. It makes it possible for us to see the need for continual growth in our Christ-life, as we become more and more aware of the varied ways in which we embody the values of the world in which we live more than those exemplified by Jesus. It helps us to take the liturgy more seriously when we pray that all who share this bread and wine may be gathered into the one body of Christ, a living sacrifice of praise.

No doubt the homily can do much to sharpen our appreciation of the liturgy's prophetic dimension. In this sense, it puts us in continuity with Christ himself. Jesus came preaching. "This is the time of fulfillment. The kingdom of God is at hand. Repent, and believe in the gospel" (Mk 1:15). Jesus looked forward to the long-promised messianic age in which God's covenant promises would be a reality. His call to change was as radical as it was demanding.

Jesus' preaching caused him to be regarded as a rabbi or a prophet. When Jesus questioned his disciples as to what people were saying about him, they could answer mainly that he was a prophet, like John the Baptist or Elijah. His own disciples confessed that they thought him to be "a prophet mighty in deed and word" (Lk 24:19). The prophetic aspect of Jesus' teaching was very apparent to his hearers.

Preaching—even poor preaching—is like a story within a story. Any gospel passage is part of a larger story: a story of God with his people Israel. That plot begins with the call of Abraham and moves forward to its climax in God's own Word-made-flesh. Even this is a component of the still larger story of God and humanity. This story takes us from the creation to a vision of a new heaven and a new earth. We move from the promise of the Holy Spirit, who has gone from brooding over the waters of chaos to completing the work of Christ in the age that is yet to come.

Because we believe Jesus to have been truly human, he is preached and understood as a character in the story of humanity. In focusing on Jesus' humanity, we see his story as our story as well. Christ is linked to our own historical reality. Understanding Jesus is the clue to understanding the whole human story. Jesus is central to the meaning and direction of human history itself.

Since Vatican II we have begun to take the humanity of Christ more seriously. Jerome Murphy-O'Connor, in *Becoming Human Together*, develops the implications of this basic insight from the standpoint of Pauline theology. Older spirituality spoke as if human life were basically sinful. Even today, there is an expression in Filipino (and probably many other languages as well) that one often hears after someone confesses wrongdoing: "What can you expect? I'm only human." The implication is that the human level is necessarily characterized by sin and evil.

In this conception, the coming of Jesus altered the equation by bringing us the reality of grace, which takes us from the natural (sinful) level, and raises us to the supernatural level. Here, of course, life is bathed in the grace of the Spirit, and we are able to perform meritorious acts and be pleasing to God.

Unfortunately, there seems to be no warrant in the scriptures for two such levels. In St. Paul we have a tremendous development of the idea that Christ Jesus is the perfect human being. If we want to know what our humanity is capable of doing—and what God wants it to do—we need only look to Christ. Jesus is the embodiment of what God intended all of his creation to be from the very beginning.

By embodying the fullness of humanity, Christ enables us to appreciate what it means to be human. Thus Iraeneus' famous statement that "the glory of God is a fully alive human being." There is no need to be boosted to some higher level to be virtuous. We need only actualize the potentialities of our own humanness. Everything we hear about Jesus becomes a challenge for our own self-understanding and growth. To be sinful is not to be human, it is to abdicate what humanity is all about and lower ourselves to the level of the animals.

This understanding of Christ draws us beyond our present vistas to a future vision of what can be, and what God desires. We often speak of the eucharist as a foretaste of the messianic banquet in the heavenly kingdom. This is simply a way of saying that the eucharist is not the ultimate reality. Rather, it points to an as yet unfulfilled future when God will be all in all.

So, in the liturgy, we gather, we preach, and we break bread. But by trying to understand the larger picture of God's dealing with his universe, each celebration is a prayer that we might be faithful to what God has already accomplished in history and everything that the eucharist points to and claims to celebrate.

However, it is not only the scriptures or the homily that issues a prophetic challenge for all of us. So does the entire liturgy. The very gathering of the community is already a prophetic statement. For here we find rich and poor, young and old; here there is no longer Jew nor Greek, male nor female. The fact that people who would not otherwise associate with one another at work or at play can be found so easily at the same table is a powerful affirmation of the power of the Holy Spirit to transform us. It is also a statement about human dignity and whence it derives.

The eucharistic prayer also is prophetic. Having gathered and heard the scriptures and praised God for the marvels he has worked in our world and that he has accomplished for us in Christ, we pray that the Holy Spirit might go about her work of transformation. This prayer to the Spirit is always expressed in terms of the transformation needed to bring about the unity of the community. We also ask for the transformation of the bread and wine that we have brought to the altar. And, by implication at least, we also ask for the transformation of the world in which we live, so that creation itself might be set free from slavery to corruption and share in the glorious freedom of the children of God (Rom 8:19-23).

In invoking the Holy Spirit, we plead that "we all may be brought together in unity by the Holy Spirit." Or, as the third eucharistic prayer puts it, "Grant that we, who are nourished by [Christ's] body and blood, may be filled with his Holy Spirit, and become one body, one spirit in Christ." In this regard, the new eucharistic prayers are all patterned after the earliest known prayers of the church. These all recognized that life in the Spirit would bring us together.

The earliest known eucharistic prayer we have, from the *Didache,* comes from the first century. In it this insight about oneness is linked to the element of the gifts placed on the altar. There we pray that "as this broken bread was once scattered on the hillsides and was gathered together and made one, so let your church be gathered together into your kingdom from the ends of the earth." This insight was a constant feature of the preaching of the Fathers.

As noted in Chapter 2, however, our prayer to the Holy Spirit has been curiously divided in our present liturgies. Having begun by asking that the Spirit transform the gifts, we pause to recall the institution narrative. Only later do we resume to ask for the transformation of the community into Christ's true ecclesial body. This makes it too easy for us to assume that all is well as long as the bread and wine become the body and blood of Christ, forgetting that we are also asking for a like transformation of the celebrating community.

In this regard, it might be good to recall that the signs of the eucharist go beyond the bread and the wine. Those who celebrate are also part of the sign. Because the eucharist is an action, not some static reality, we might even say they are the most important part of the sign. Obviously, if the community is one, and making an conscious effort to be true to the gospel and to grow in the knowledge and love of God, then the eucharist will be powerful and prophetic.

It is doubtful, however, that the exigencies of the gospel and the liturgy will ever be borne by us if we do not cultivate the awareness of the transformative element in the eucharist. This may require a fresh new way of regarding the eucharistic liturgy. This is something each of us can and must do.

We should begin by realizing that it is *our* bread and wine that is placed on the altar, our lives, so that the Spirit might transform our human dying into the glory of new life. As we have mentioned already, there is no need to presuppose that all those who celebrate the eucharist are ready for canonization. The reality is that all those at the altar are in need of healing and of God's grace. All are broken in various ways, whether by reason of sin, or because of the circumstances of their lives.

Eucharist, however, dares to make the assertion that it is not power that rules the world, but powerlessness. Those who exercised power were able to put Jesus to death. But the powerlessness of Christ triumphed over the powers of this world. It is this ultimate paradox that we proclaim each time that we celebrate. Success in the eyes of God is very different from success in the eyes of the world.

The various problems that beset all who gather to celebrate the liturgy are characteristic of God's people. Nevertheless, we are enabled to lay our brokenness on the altar and know that it will be as acceptable as the gift of Christ himself. Not only that, but the very brokenness we bring can and will be transformed according to the pattern of Christ's own death.

The prophetic aspect of the eucharist is somewhat like a stretching exercise. It challenges us to use muscles that have long lain dormant, to reach beyond what has become customary. It affords us a glimpse of the future, of what can (and should) be. It is this vision of a better world that allows us to struggle for that time when there are no more tears, no more suffering, when God will come to vindicate the just.

A final realization that should be ours if the eucharist is to be truly prophetic is that each time we say "Amen" to the eucharistic prayer or to the body of Christ, we are acknowledging that we accept everything that Jesus stood for. If we do so, we are also making a personal commitment to change, to grow in the life of the Spirit. This commitment is not simply a personal one. It is a commitment to grow with and for each other.

Lest this seem a normal conclusion, we should keep in mind that the present legislation of the church forbids reception of the sacraments to those who are "in the state of sin." This includes the divorced and remarried, and a number of others whose actions have put them outside the discipline of the church. The implication behind this way of thinking, of course, is that the eucharist is a reward for the just.

Who is just, however? There are two problems here. One is that we all tend to judge ourselves on the same scale. Sin becomes a concrete reality that is the same for all. I am convinced, however, that if God has given me ten talents, and some other poor soul only one, he is demanding of me ten times more (if not a hundred). To think that we can come up with one universal scale that will judge everyone is ridiculous.

Another problem with this understanding is that it bases itself on the ten commandments. Though I am not advocating getting rid of the commandments, the problem with them is that the morality there is strictly personal. There is nothing there of social justice. Lacking also is any thought of a hierarchy of evils, or of the existence of structural evils, or of sin as being something larger than ourselves. All of this is woefully inadequate today.

What each eucharist should reinforce in each of those who participate is a commitment to growth, to development, to a deep realization we are all fall short of the grace offered us by God.

7

With Open Eyes:
Reading the Signs of the Times

Let the people of Zion exult in their king.
Let them praise his name in the dance,
and sing psalms to him with tambourine and lyre,
for the Lord accepts the service of his people.
—Psalm 149:2-4

In 1832 Félicité de Lamennais was condemned in two encyclicals of Gregory XVI for advocating freedom of conscience and the separation of church and state. Vatican II adopted both of these positions. In the decade before that council, people like John Courtney Murray, Henri de Lubac, Yves Congar, Pierre Chenu, Teilhard de Chardin, even Karl Rahner were silenced by Rome. All of them emerged as either *periti* (advisors) or as lights by which the council guided itself.

Today we notice similar silencings: Hans Kung, Charles Curran, Leonardo Boff, Bishop Pedro Casaldaliga, and others. Will they emerge as visionaries of the future? It is not always easy to tell. But such has ever been the lot of prophets, who will ever remain the most fascinating, yet perhaps the most irritating of people.

Prophets are fascinating because they are willing to stand up for what they believe, even in the face of opposition or persecution. Through the ages they have stood for truth and integrity. Because they proclaim a prophetic word, a God-word for people today, challenging accepted ideas, they are considered dangerous by vested interests. Their ideas are very difficult to stop. People can be silenced; ideas have a life of their own.

Few of us would consider ourselves prophets. Perhaps we would never aspire to be one, either. It suffices, however, to be committed to the truth to be prophetic. Only a few are called to go beyond this to be public signs of contradiction in the world.

This latter group is what we tend to think of when we consider prophets. They have managed to irk the powers that be, and many of them have suffered for their efforts, even to being killed. One need only think of the careers of Amos, Jeremiah, Jesus, Oscar Romero— to name but a few.

We might mention in the United States someone like Daniel Berrigan, who has spent close to half his life in jail for pouring blood on draft records, or breaking into nuclear facilities and pounding rocket nose cones with little hammers. Whether we agree with his stand or his tactics, the fact remains that he is performing an important service to the rest of the community. He is willing to stand up and tell the rest of us that war— especially nuclear war—is total madness, that it is no way to solve the world's problems. Were no one to do this, the world would be the poorer.

We should all aspire to be prophets. We may not feel moved to take stands that will command national attention, but our integrity requires that we do so on a personal level. At least in our own homes, in our work, or in our social circles, we are called to stand for right.

The prophetic God-word challenges the smug assumptions of any given age and culture. Most people are so caught up in their society and culture that they do not have the perspective to question its basic suppositions. Two hundred years ago even religious orders owned slaves. They thought themselves virtuous if they treated them humanely. Because they were so immersed in their culture, they were unable to criticize this inhuman institution.

The task of prophets is to provide the perspective that so many lack. It is to raise questions no one else thinks to ask. Prophets bring a fresh approach to God's word, so that it can be applied to current situations in new and creative ways, ways that help us to be more faithful to what God is about.

God's word calls us beyond our present vistas to a future vision of what can and should be. The liturgy takes in all periods of time. If we are to be faithful to what God has already accomplished in our history, and to what the eucharist claims to celebrate now, as well as what the Holy Spirit hopes to accomplish, we need to grasp that vision of the *parousia* that will keep us on the proper track. Prophets make this possible.

Not all prophets were killed. Some were even successful in their own time. If we need a model of a successful prophet to follow, I would suggest Nathan. Nathan was not one of those sycophantic types, seeking only to please those in power. In fact, when the king of Israel committed adultery with Uriah's wife and then compounded this sin by sending Uriah off to his death in battle, Nathan confronted him with his wrongdoing.

Perhaps it is fortunate that Nathan was dealing with King David. Nevertheless, Nathan was too shrewd simply to blurt out that the king was an adulterer and a murderer. Instead, he told him a parable. In the parable he described how a poor man having only one sheep was despoiled of it by a rich man in the same town, though this latter had entire fields of sheep of his own. Hearing this, David grew angry and declared that the man who did this deserved to die and should repay the poor man fourfold.

This was the moment that Nathan was waiting for. Leveling his finger at David, he declared, "You are that man!" David was honest enough to realize that Nathan had been sent by God. Instead of doing away with the messenger, he acknowledged that what Nathan said was all too true. Accepting the fact of his guilt, he was willing to atone and to rebuild his relationship with God.

There are three elements here that should be noted for all who would be prophets. First, there was the perception of a wrong. Nathan knew that David had sinned. It did not matter that other potentates in the Near East at that time could sleep with any woman in the realm with impunity. David was under the covenant, and what he did was evil. Nathan was also astute enough to make David aware of the fact that a wrong had been done. He did so in such a way that David accepted it even when he realized that he himself was the author of the wrongdoing.

Second, Nathan issued a call for repentance, a change of heart. David admitted that he had sinned. He was willing to accept punishment. He repented and was willing to convert. Conversion was a requirement laid down by Jesus when he invited us to enter the kingdom and believe the good news of salvation. This is what makes possible the third and final step: renewing and deepening our relationship with God.

Ultimately, it is our relationship with God that is at stake here. It is the voice of the prophets that call us to be faithful. Left to ourselves we are too prone to self-deception, or to the blindness that comes from over-familiarity. The prophetic voice challenges us to rethink our priorities, to ask where we are going, continually to reassess our values and ways of acting.

The prophetic aspect of our prayer serves as a constant reminder that as followers of Christ we are called to change the world rather than be changed by it. This implies a specific way of thinking, an active effort to translate fidelity into loving behavior. With Walter Brueggeman, we might list seven aspects of the prophetic task.

First is the ability to read the signs of the times. Pope John XXIII linked this with the work of Vatican II, and it should be clear that it is a skill that should always characterize us. What is implied here is the readiness and willingness to make critical evaluations of the world in which we live. It is a question of bringing the gospel to bear on the reality of our universe, on the problems that afflict society. We need vision to see what is actually happening around us so that we are not simply carried on through life at the mercy of whatever forces are around us.

Another requirement is to be sensitive to the pain and suffering around us. Though evil and injustice seem to be everywhere, for many they are still abstract, not really felt. Most people are not genuinely aware of the needs of others. In Studs Terkel's book *Race*, one of the more interesting quotations is from a man who was once an Exalted Cyclops of the Ku Klux Klan. By some fluke he was named to a community relations board and came face to face with blacks for the first time in his life. This experience was so moving that this bigoted racist became a rather successful civil rights activist.

Once we have read the signs of the times with sensitivity, we are able to articulate alternative futures for ourselves. This requires the willingness to question the assumptions of our age and culture. This need not be an iconoclastic exercise. But there is a sense in which we should approach all of life with a healthy dose of skepticism. We need to resist the law of inertia whereby things remain the same because "they have always been that way." A little imagination may reveal ways of doing things that are better, more just, or humane.

Alternative futures do not drop out of trees. They have to be sought after, studied and planned, implemented and evaluated. Sadly, suggestions for change are often met with resistance, either because of inertia or vested interests. They have to be demonstrated as better or more effective before others will try them. Our suggestions have to be practical, and they must be seen to benefit us more than other alternatives—or the status quo.

A fourth aspect of the prophetic task is that it enables people to engage in history. Most people feel overwhelmed at the enormity of the bureaucracy or the impersonality of the marketplace. A prophetic life is one that provides means whereby people sense that there *is* something that can be done to make things better. In one sense, this is what the small basic Christian communities have managed to do. Real empowerment takes place, and passivity, or a sense of fatalism, is replaced with real Christian hope.

Fifth, the prophetic imagination must be in the service of justice and peace. God is said to be on the side of the oppressed, and it is precisely because of the option for the poor that any evangelization can take place. Unless our prayer and liturgy take us into the heart of the struggle for a better world, we are dreaming up for ourselves an ethereal religion that bears little resemblance to what Jesus lived and died for.

In this day and age, injustice can be (and is) fought in various ways. Ultimately, however, there will never be peace unless our struggle for justice is based on love. Anger only begets more anger, and violence spawns ever greater violence. If the dehumanizing spiral of violence is ever to be ended, it will be through love. Love, in this sense, is life's only true healing force. When Jesus said from the cross, "Father, forgive them; they do not know what they are doing," he was doing more than turning the other cheek. He was refusing to be mastered by evil, not allowing his enemies to drag him down to their own level. He was a free person.

Sixth, prophetic people also need to provide new symbols enabling people to see reality in a fresh way, allowing them to dream of what can be. We are all prisoners of our symbols. When the church is thought of as a perfect society, with the main emphasis on the institution, we have a very different idea of the church and its ministry than if we see it as a community of disciples or as a prophetic force. Changing the symbols changes the way we see the reality.

Finally, prophets are able to foster hope in a new future. There will be a new heaven and a new earth. The old has passed away (cf. Rv 21:1-4). In those days God himself will wipe every tear from our eyes. There is a whole world of possibilities that lies just beyond our grasp. Like children with noses pressed to the storefront, admiring all the things they would like to have, hope presses our noses to the window of the future and lets us see what we are called to be.

In Dominique Lapierre's *City of Joy* the point is made that even with the poorest of the poor in Calcutta's slums, there was a difference between the Christians and the Hindus. Somehow the Christians were better off. In part this was because, not having the fatalism of the Hindus, they were more willing to do something to change and improve their situation. They had hope that things could be otherwise.

If we allow the liturgy to give us a prophetic sensitivity, our lives will take on added importance and meaning. We will realize the tremendous power that is ours as a force for good. There are various ways to go about this. We should be looking for ways to be more effective, keeping our goals firmly in mind and seeking the best ways to accomplish them.

I know a priest who, for his very first homily in a new parish, looked the people in the eye and announced "I haven't come here to comfort the afflicted; I've come to afflict the comfortable." And that he did. But because the people felt he had judged them and found them wanting even before he had gotten to know them, his manner almost brought about a revolution in that parish, and the bishop soon had to replace him.

So many self-appointed prophets are like that. We must remember that love is the only ultimate force for transformation. We cannot criticize people we do not love and expect them to respond positively to our approach. The nature of the gospel requires a loving approach. Prophets are not guaranteed success, but they do not have to doom their own efforts by alienating the very ones they hope to change.

Assuming that we want to walk with open eyes, to be able to read the signs of the times, for what should we be especially alert? For most people opportunities will be suggested in the workplace, the social arena, or the home. And in each of these, a correct line of action is not something we can map out in advance. Situations vary, individual talents are unique, and much will depend on our ability to read the signs of the times. We all need to become more aware of the circumstances in which we live, to see how we might respond to current needs and bring the gospel to bear on our world.

In 1991 the church celebrated one hundred years of Catholic social thought. Beginning with Leo XIII's encyclical *Rerum novarum*, there has been increased emphasis on the social application of the gospel. The Second Vatican Council gave us a landmark document *Gaudium et spes*. And recent popes, beginning with John XXIII, have issued encyclicals and pronouncements dealing with social questions. Bishops' conferences have also made major statements, for example, the United States bishops' documents on nuclear war and on the economy.

What comes out of these documents, aside from specific courses of action, are major themes or guiding principles for Christian action in the world. We cannot pretend to be faithful to the rhythms of the eucharist if we ignore them. Let us list some of these principles:

The social and religious dimensions of life are linked. The social is not secular, in the sense of being outside God's plan. Faith and justice are two sides of the same coin. There is no dichotomy between religion and reality, between liturgy and life. Being holy requires that our prayer results in action. As the 1971 synod put it, the promotion of justice is a constitutive element of the proclamation of the gospel.

Each human being shares the same dignity. All men and women are made in the image and likeness of God.

As such they have a preeminent place in the social order and enjoy inalienable rights that need respect and defense. The poor are not inferior to the rich and the powerful in this regard. All human creatures have a beauty that can (and should) mirror the divine for us. Hence the evil of those "isms" that polarize and divide—sexism, racism, consumerism, and so on. By categorizing people we no longer see them as individuals and effectively dehumanize them.

Christians should have a preferential option for the poor. The needs and rights of the poor were given special attention by Jesus. It was that sector of humanity with which he most closely identified. In many third-world countries this is being done by means of basic ecclesial communities. These communities enable people to base their lives more closely on the gospel, empower them to recognize their own dignity and worth, and help them improve their own lot. In the First World we need to be more aware of how the desire for profits leads to exploitation, keeping people in a spiral of poverty from which it is almost impossible to emerge.

The common good should be promoted. In an era of rank individualism, we need to be reminded of the importance of the common good. Men and women can more easily attain the perfection of their humanity when the economic, cultural, and political situation is just and does not cater to special interests. In determining policies we should try to do the greatest good for the greatest number. We are, in a real sense, our brothers' and sisters' keepers.

We are stewards of the earth's goods. For years we took too literally the injunction in Genesis that we fill the earth and subdue it, having dominion over the rest of the creatures. This has led to the rape of the land, to mortgaging the future for the sake of immediate gain. It has resulted in exploitation on a global scale, so that only a small percentage of the earth's people control the majority of the earth's wealth and resources. Today we have to worry about the greenhouse effect, whether America will agree to reductions of gas emissions, the gradual extinction of fish populations, the worldwide effect of the exploitation of the Brazilian rain forest, the poisoning of the land by pesticides and fertilizers, and on and on. We are stewards, and we will be called to give an account of our stewardship.

We are all linked globally. If the space age allows us to speak of earth as a global village, it is equally true that we are all linked as members of the same human family. As such we have mutual obligations to promote the development and well-being of peoples across the world. In one sense this is but an acknowledgment of our common dependence on God. The idea of a world order, or the general concept of the United Nations, is more than a political expedient; it is the direction indicated by the Holy Spirit.

All should participate in the political order. People should have a say in their own destiny. Decisions affecting the lives of millions should not be made without allowing them to participate in the process. It is easy to exploit and disenfranchise the weak and powerless, whether they be the poor, certain races, women, minorities, or laity in the church. What we are seeking here is a deeper respect for the dignity of all God's people, not a simplistic espousal of so-called democracy.

All should work at promoting peace. Ultimately, peace is the fruit of justice and is dependent on a right order among human beings as well as among nations. The dominant model that seems to govern the relations among peoples today is a competitive one. We need to seek more cooperative ways of living together. Developing a consistent ethic of life and a deep concern of how to live together in the global village is a necessity if we are to survive.

These are some of the areas that demand Christian attention. If we can see the liturgy as a prophetic action, then we will realize that we cannot go through life with our eyes closed to the evil and sin around us. Rather, by reading the signs of the times, we can discern how we can use our own talents and gifts to make this a world where Christ's values rule—not only in our lives, but in the society in which we live. Then we can joyfully praise God's name in song and dance, as we offer him our service as his people.

8

The Nurturing Rhythm

They cut me down
and I leapt up high.
I am the life
that'll never, never die.
I'll live in you
if you'll live in me.
I am the Lord
of the dance, said he.

The communion rite brings the liturgy of the eucharist to a close. We have come a long way in recent years as regards communion. Not much more than a hundred years ago St. Thérèse had to be given special permission from her confessor to receive communion daily. The rest of her Carmelite sisters had to content themselves with monthly or weekly reception. There was such a stress on our personal unworthiness that communion was a rare event in the lives of most people.

Though Pius X succeeded in making frequent communion once again a reality in the church, this action had already begun to achieve independent status, apart from the liturgy. Pious souls would arrive at church in time to receive communion and use the next mass in "thanksgiving" for this gift of the Lord. Communion was sometimes distributed before the mass for the same reason. In larger churches, priests would come out after the consecration (if not earlier) and begin distributing communion to the faithful, while the priest at the altar continued on his merry way. Unless it was a later mass, of course. Then the eucharistic fast (from midnight in those days) assured that only a dozen or so would receive out of an assembly of several hundred.

Vatican II enabled us to see communion once again as an integral part of the liturgy of the eucharist. Our bread and wine are returned to us transformed, a gift from the hand of God. The growing custom of consecrating the bread needed at each eucharist as well as the practice of communion under both species also helps tie the eucharistic liturgy together as one act of corporate worship. The vast majority of the community now shares in communion. The use of eucharistic ministers has also helped reduce the over-sacralization of communion.

We still have not reached the *parousia*, however, as far as communion is concerned. It continues to be misunderstood, separated from the liturgy which prepares it, and often reduced to a popular devotion. The real problem may be that for many people it is still essentially a Jesus-and-me reality. Having received the eucharistic gifts we can shut out the rest of the congregation and immerse ourselves in silent conversation with Christ. It becomes our moment alone with Jesus. Whether there are two or two thousand others there makes little difference.

This is not to deny that in communion we are nourished with the very body and blood of Christ, or that we have communion with him in the eucharist. In every mass, having given its "amen" to the eucharistic prayer, the community is fed by the Jesus himself. The natural conclusion of the liturgy of the eucharist is sharing in communion. Jesus does not invite us to his table only to admire the food. He desires that we partake at his table, that we eat his body and drink his blood so that we might have true life.

The church has gone out of its way, especially after the Second Vatican Council, to assure that we do not mistake the meaning of this rite and of the life we receive. It did this by the simple expedient of adding the kiss of peace. The liturgical commission that prepared the changes had a choice of several locations for this ritual, all of which have some precedent in our history.

It could have been placed at the beginning of the mass, where it would have functioned as a sort of greeting, a recognition of those with whom were are about to pray and worship.

Or, it could have come after the liturgy of the word. Many ancient liturgies have it at this point, where it served as a seal on the proclamation of the gospel, a sort of mutual pledge or commitment to its message. In the days of the catechumenate, since both catechumens and penitents were dismissed just before this, it drove home the point that they were not yet worthy to exchange this "pure Christian kiss." For Christians, the kiss of peace was a sign of deep solidarity in the work of Christ. Beyond encouraging one another to live the message of the gospel after the homily, it was a sort of guarantee of the genuineness of the celebration. It recalled the gospel passage that reminds us that if we are bringing our gift to the altar and remember that anyone has something against us, we should leave our gift and go be reconciled before offering it (Mt 5:24).

Or, they could have chosen the end of the mass, where the kiss found itself at the beginning of the fourth century. As people greeted one another before leaving the church, it served as an assent to all that had preceded and a sign of mutual encouragement in living the fullness of what they had just celebrated.

The commission chose, however, to place it at the beginning of the communion rite, immediately after the Our Father, where it had lodged itself more or less since the time of Gregory the Great. In so doing the commission deliberately put the emphasis on the petition of the Lord's Prayer whereby we ask that we be forgiven as we in turn forgive those who have injured us. It thus serves as an immediate preparation for the worthy reception of communion.

This emphasizes the original intent. In some periods in the early church those not receiving communion were not even given the kiss. Instead they were dismissed. Those remaining then exchanged the kiss and went on to receive communion.

Unfortunately, prior to the council, we seldom saw this ritual except at solemn high masses. And then it was only exchanged by those in the sanctuary—not as a personal, heartfelt exchange, but as a stylized and somewhat formal shadow of its former self.

The following story comes from a priest who was chairman of the liturgical commission in the Philippines at the time when the new ritual was being put into use. He recounts that the members of the commission had been going around the country trying to prepare people to understand and appreciate the new ritual. After a day-long explanation to catechists and lay leaders, there was an actual demonstration of the new mass. When they got to the kiss of peace, which was something quite new, he remembers saying something like, "And now, please give a sign of peace in whatever way you see fit to those around you." As he himself turned to do so to the servers, he heard a slight commotion in the back of the church, and the sound of someone crying. It was only after the mass was over and he was back in the sacristy that he found out what had happened.

A sister came in and apologized for having caused the incident. It seems that she was in the same pew with another sister with whom she had not spoken in two years. When the invitation came to give the sign of peace, feeling herself unable, she moved up several pews instead. It was the one abandoned in the pew who had cried. Father's answer was simple, "Why did you bother going to communion?" A very important question.

What is the meaning of communion if one is living a life of alienation? Communion is an act of solidarity with the entire community. Yet, few of the communion prayers that we see in missals and prayer books reinforce this truth. Even our language betrays us. We speak of "receiving" or "going to" communion. It is as if communion were an act of personal piety rather than a gift to all God's people gathered precisely as members of one family. It is a sharing that we receive in common and which, in some mysterious way, includes all others.

Two things that happened to the ritual at this point may have helped privatize communion. One was the disappearance of the fraction rite. The fraction prayers were eloquent about the unity of the community. They urged us to become one just as the bread is made up of many grains or the wine results from the crushing of many grapes. If these could be the body of Christ, we also become his true body in sharing with our brothers and sisters.

Later piety added two prayers for the priest at this point, prayers that are still in the ritual. The priest is

supposed to choose one. Since many priests (mistaken-
ly) say these aloud, they are familiar to most Catholics.
The first asks for deliverance from all sin and for the
grace to be faithful to Christ's teaching. The second asks
that the reception of the eucharist may work not to one's
condemnation, but to health of mind and body. Taken
alone, both are rather individualistic. It would be more
helpful to hear something about becoming one with all
the other members of Christ's body.

While personal union with Jesus is essential to a
deeply Christian life, such a union is deficient if it fails
to take in the totality of the risen Christ. Communion
with Jesus is a communion in the *whole* Christ, body and
members. We cannot arbitrarily decide to have fewer
brothers or sisters than Jesus himself does. Our communion is not simply with the risen Lord, but with his
entire body. This is the union, the *koinonia* that Jesus
prayed for the night before he died.

We mistake the meaning of communion if we approach the holy table with our hands out only to receive.
Jesus shares himself with us so that we might have
something worthwhile to share with one another. The
nurturing rhythm speaks not so much about our being
fed, but of our being empowered to feed each other, to
become a truly nurturing community. Communion
should result in a true nurturing in love, justice, and
peace. Eucharist is meant to enable the church to sense
more deeply its communion and what it means to be the
body of Christ.

Saying "amen!" when the communion minister
offers us the body and blood of Christ is not simply an
act of faith in the reality of Jesus' presence in the bread
and wine. It is an act of commitment and solidarity to
everything that Jesus is and stands for. It asks to be a

more fruitful member of his body as we incarnate his own love and compassion in the world today. All this is done not with fellow saints, but with fellow sinners.

Over the years the church has struggled with two different concepts of what the church really is. There has always been the temptation to think that we are meant to be a church of the perfect, that those who are sinners should be removed and made to realize the evil of their ways. Thus we have employed excommunications and have even been willing to enforce virtue by means of the Inquisition. We still insist that none of those in the state of sin should approach the table of the eucharist.

Eventually, however, we came to realize that the gospels had it right all along. There we read the parable of the net thrown into the sea coming up with all sorts of fish. Or we recall the parable of the weeds among the wheat, which the master prefers to sort out only at harvest time. The church is and will remain a "mixed bag." We are all imperfect; we are all sinners. But this is a blessing.

There is something arrogant about the former notion. It enabled some of us to line up for communion and look down our noses at those still in the pew, imagining ourselves better than our sinful brethren who were left behind. But there is something wrong about judging anyone to begin with. None of us will be judged on the same scale as our neighbor. How can people use some external scale to convince themselves that they are one of the just, while ranking others with the unjust? We have a hard enough time trying to appreciate and be faithful to the gifts and talents God has given each of us. Yet, this will be the ultimate criterion: our own gifts and graces, not those of others, or any standard devised by others. We will be judged by God on how well we have corresponded to what we have received from him.

Our understanding of sin is woefully inadequate. A current examination of conscience in an *Opus Dei* missal takes up five whole pages. Small type, too. Minute questioning on the various commandments (especially the sixth) is there in enough quantity to please the most scrupulous. There is not one mention about anything having to do with social justice, however. There is practically nothing about acts of omission, the failures of Christians to put into practice the faith that is ours as Christ would have us live it. Sin is treated as an individualistic reality; no thought is given to structural or social sin. Is there not something strange about the mentality that allows us to exclude those who are divorced and remarried from communion, while ushering up to the altar rail those tycoons of industry who may have caused untold harm to others by shady business practices or white-collar crimes that seldom are named for what they are? Why do we show such selectivity about what we term sin?

One of the conditions necessary if we are to be truly fed by the Lord is that we acknowledge our own inadequacy, our desperate need for Christ's bread. The Christian community, in fact, is not a place where hunger, thirst, and neediness are exceptional. These are our characteristics! We are a sinful, pilgrim people. And there are two other conditions that must be fulfilled if we are to become a truly nurturing church.

The first is that we must know what it means to feed one another. This condition is relatively easy. For centuries the church has been known for its works of charity. Feeding the poor has characterized the church from the beginning. Even in the summary statements in

Acts (2:42ff and 4:32ff) we note the stress on the fact that there were no poor among them, because people used to sell their possessions in order to care for others.

Through the ages countless hospitals, schools, and other social services requiring huge expenditures have marked the church's efforts to care for others. Although we may tend to leave this work to others, we do acknowledge its importance, and we are grateful that someone else is doing it. Our own efforts may be on the more prosaic level of the neighbor next door, the sick person down the street, or the persons we work with. All this is good. Any cup of cold water given in Christ's name is worthwhile.

Yet all of us need to note the need and pain of others, to reach out to those that no one else seems to care about. There are so many neglected people in the world, those we pass and hardly notice despite the fact that we pass them each day. At communion time we pray that we develop better sight to notice what is lacking to our world.

The second condition is more difficult than the first. To do a good job caring for others, we must also know what it is to be fed by others. We are much more willing to lend a helping hand where others are concerned than to admit our own need for help. Acknowledging our own neediness implies a dependency, a helplessness we would rather not experience. Were Jesus to feed us from the cross, we would be happy; that he wills to do so through another we tend to see as a diminishment.

This may explain the popularity of the book *The Wounded Healer*. Henri Nouwen makes us realize that neediness applies to everyone; beginning with Christ, we are all wounded healers. Being aware of our own weaknesses should make us better able to understand and minister to the weaknesses of others.

These conditions, then, are all necessary if we are to be truly nurtured by the eucharist.

St. John's gospel gives no account of communion or of the institution of the eucharist. Most likely this is because by the end of the first century, he was already aware of the real problem with many eucharists. Despite our celebrations, and the number of times communion is received, the active, self-giving love of God fails to become a reality in our lives. St. John thought it necessary to stress the washing of the feet at the last supper with its stark reminder: "I have given you an example . . . so must you do."

Interestingly enough, we have never attempted to ritualize this action except on Holy Thursday. But Jesus' action goes far beyond any ritual. And his telling us that we should all imitate the example he has given us means more than that we should be willing to perform even the most menial tasks for one another. His action tells us that to the degree we have been filled and transformed by the self-giving love of Christ for us, we should be eager to live out a similar gift of self toward one another.

Just as Peter recognized the need for total cleansing, so should we. Jesus' actions symbolize the complete change that is needed in our way of thinking, a stripping away of all earthly values in order to live as he lived. His was a life filled with the power of the Holy Spirit, with concern for the poor, and with a desire to free those under bondage. It was the life of one totally committed to being a source of mercy and compassion in the world.

Perhaps we will never reach this point unless we once again eat actual bread for communion and really drink from the chalice of Christ's blood. Communion under both species, an essential and important element of the sign, might strike people more forcefully with the realization that the reality of communion is far richer than we had previously imagined. Jesus gives us far more than we can chew. Though given to us personally, this banquet is for the entire community, which is to be transformed as a result of the eucharistic celebration.

The Fathers of the Eastern Church often linked the reception of Christ's blood with the action of the Holy Spirit. It was the Spirit that made the blood life-giving, that made it possible for us to be joined to the total Christ in oneness of life and love. This is far more concrete and life-producing than simply saying that we receive an increase of grace!

Grace is too impersonal a concept. Rather, we must come to see that communion makes us become one with Christ himself in a loving union of life that is as real as that which exists among the Father, the Spirit, and the Son. It also breaks down whatever barriers separate us one from another. We all share the same life. As the song reminds us, Jesus will live in us if we are willing to live in him—in the whole Christ, head and members. He is the Lord of the dance.

"For in one Spirit we were all baptized into one body," says St. Paul. "We were all given to drink of one Spirit. Now the body is not a single part, but many" (1 Cor 12:13). May communion enable us to drink in Christ's Spirit in plentiful draughts and be filled with a new infusion of trinitarian life. Then, just as we are able to recognize that the bread and wine we offered has been changed and transformed, we may look anew at our brother or sister and see beyond the veil to recognize the face of Christ himself.

9

With Open Hands: Involvement

Girls will then dance for joy,
and men young and old will rejoice.
I shall turn their grief into gladness,
comfort them and give them joy after sorrow,
and my people will have their fill of my bounty.
—*Jeremiah 31:13-14*

One day in Manila I was at our downtown church. There I bumped into two little street children, aged about seven and nine. They were sisters. Home for them was an alley between two office buildings. I knew that they came from a larger family, and that they had no father—which is probably why they enjoyed being held and hugged, or otherwise given attention. On my way to the store for some medicine, I invited them to accompany me.

Fortunately, the medicine cost less than expected, so I had a bit of change left over. I gave the girls a choice: "What would you prefer, ice cream or an apple?" Apples were then selling for about thirty-five cents, about half the price of ice cream. Their eyes lit up and they both chorused, "Apples!" They had probably never had one before.

I bought each of them a nice big apple. They held them out, almost in admiration, all the way back to the church. At length I asked, "Aren't you going to eat them?" Their answer still leaves me ashamed. "No," they said. "We're going to bring them home to share with our brothers and sisters." I myself would probably have succumbed to the temptation to eat the apple and say nothing about it at home. They saw sharing not as a burden, but as an opportunity, a privilege, a joy. These two uneducated children knew more about sharing and eucharist than I did.

This is how Jesus would have us share. Sharing is what eucharist is all about. Jesus not only shares himself with us, but gives us the example and strength to share with one another. Eucharist is how Christ continues to nurture his church. If we want to see how the eucharist is expected to be lived out in real life, we can do no better than to ponder the pattern of life we see reflected in the miraculous feeding stories in the gospels. They have intrigued commentators for centuries, especially because of their frankly eucharistic language. There we read that Jesus took, blessed, broke, and distributed the bread to the people. It is a perfect echo of the consecration of the mass. Deliberately so.

But not all evangelists tell the story as does St. John. In his gospel Jesus simply takes, blesses, breaks, and distributes the bread himself. In typical Johannine fashion, any middlemen have been eliminated. The disciples only collect what was left over.

The synoptics give us a slightly different account, however. The change is significant. We read in Mark 6:41, for example, that after Jesus blessed and broke the bread, he gave it *to his disciples* to distribute. This comes after their reluctance to follow his previous injunction to give the people something to eat (6:37). The disciples are needed for this task. Today, Christ's bread, his ability to nourish, is distributed mainly through disciples. Should they fail, people will go hungry.

This is why the gospels all link the feeding miracle with the eucharist. This was the most significant of Jesus' meals; after the last supper, it is the only one to be mentioned in all four gospels. It is even mentioned twice in Mark and Matthew. Rare are the events that get such complete coverage in the gospels! It seems obvious that, for the gospel writers, the compassion and outreach manifested in this event were central to a proper understanding of Christian life.

It also shows the contrast between Jesus and ourselves. When he saw the people hungry, we are told that he was moved with compassion. The disciples, on the contrary, were moved by a great irritation at the thought of having to share their little food. Their solution to the hunger they saw was to get rid of the crowd. Though this would not have satisfied anyone's need for food, it would have removed the predicament to a safe distance. Out of sight, out of mind. When we can close our eyes to a problem, we can pretend that it doesn't exist.

The lessons for us today are many and various. The first might be that nurturing is rooted in the compassion of God. It might be even better to say that it is rooted in the fact that our God *is* compassion itself. God is love, we are told by St. John, and whoever remains in love remains in God (1 Jn 4:16). This causes God to remain in us. The letter goes on to note that if anyone says, "I love God," but hates brother or sister, that person is a liar. For whoever does not love someone he has seen cannot love the God who remains unseen (4:20).

This theme of Christ's—and God's—love runs through the farewell discourse after the last supper. The one commandment that Jesus gives his followers is based simply and squarely on his love, a love which is henceforth meant to characterize all disciples (see Jn 13:34-35; 15:11-17). Love, mercy, compassion—these are presented to us as the dominant characteristics of our God. They are supposed to be reflected in like manner in the lives of all who have experienced that love.

Never in the gospel do we hear Jesus telling us to be holy as God is holy—despite the fact that we can find this injunction dozens of times in the Torah. God's holiness is a major theme in the Bible. However, holiness as such is not a theme in the gospels at all. Only once (Jn 17:11) does Jesus even mention the holiness of God. We are often told, on the other hand, to imitate God's mercy and compassion. Indeed, in the gospels, mercy and compassion replace holiness as the quest of Jesus' followers.

The heart of Jesus' ethic is the imitation of God. The quality and direction of God's actions toward us is meant to determine how we behave in relation to one another. In Matthew 18:23-35, the parable of the unmerciful servant is given specifically as a teaching on what the kingdom of heaven is to be like. Those of us who have experienced God's mercy should govern our lives by the same virtue.

In both Matthew and Luke we are given a "mercy" ethic based on the fact that our heavenly Father is merciful (See Mt 5:38-48; Lk 6:27-36). God's *hesed*, his loving mercy, is meant to become the distinguishing characteristic of God's people. The last judgment scene in Matthew (25:31-46) drives home the point that it is only when the need and pain of others has touched our hearts that we will be judged worthy of heaven.

The ability to share at the Lord's table and to experience the love of Christ for us personally becomes the continuing reminder that these blessings are to be shared. A Christian life is a life of concern for one another. A Christian is one who cares. Our caring or loving heart should be such that it distinguishes us from those who have not had a similar experience of God's love.

In Acts, when Luke sets out to depict the uniqueness of the early church, we see the first "converts" coming in on the day of Pentecost. They responded to Peter's sermon by a conversion of life and accepted baptism into this new way. Thenceforth they were to be characterized by their ability to teach as the apostles did, as well as to pray, celebrate eucharist, and live a life of deep fellowship, even to holding all things in common because they were concerned for each one's need (Acts 2:42-47).

Fellowship—*koinonia*—and eucharist are mutually reinforcing realities. One flows from the other. They reinforce one another. Conversely, the absence or weakness of one adversely affects the other. In communion, we receive all from Christ. Eucharistic people are caring. But how is that caring to be exercised practically? Our examinations of conscience in this regard should perhaps take in three concentric circles. In the center one would be our relationships with family and friends. The next circle would include our neighbor, perhaps best seen as those we meet and are responsible for in our church or civic community. The third circle would include those in the larger world in which we also live. Each of these should benefit from our concern.

The first circle, surprisingly, might prove the most difficult. It is sometimes easier to be compassionate to others than it is to exercise the same concern within our own family circle. There is so much emotional investment in our own families that we have a difficult time being objective. We have so many expectations of family members that when they do not measure up there is hurt and pain, often so deep that understanding, reconciliation, and forgiveness become next to impossible.

Our society fills us with false expectations of what to expect from one another. We tend to believe the songs that others are there to "light up our lives." Unfortunately, this implies also the converse—that they are able to, and often do, darken them as well. If we have succumbed to the temptation to notice whatever is wrong rather than what is right with others as well, we are programmed for disaster.

One writer speaks tellingly of "the mystery of evil which good people do." Nowhere is that more true than in families. The amount of negligence and abuse that children take, the number of marriages that are unhappy or that end in divorce, the feuds among family members are sufficient witness to the fact that there is a need for a continuing family apostolate. This should be our first area of concern.

At the root of the problem is a preoccupation with self. People expect others to make them feel good. But when people do not measure up to our expectations, we begin to wonder what is wrong with them (not with ourselves, of course). The more we think about this, the worse we feel, until we begin to objectify what's wrong in the other person. What is so often lacking here, however, is genuine communication. People talk *at* each other, but often at cross purposes. They lack the ability to hear (because they do not really care) what the other person is saying.

To undo this evil, it might help if we were to make a conscious effort to increase love and self-worth in the members of our families. Of course, this should characterize our approach with others as well. This requires that all our actions be scrutinized to see whether they are truly life-giving for others. Our conversation and dialogue must aim at understanding and appreciating others, not at converting them to our way of thinking or practice. We really do not treat others as persons unless we give them the same freedom and autonomy that we expect from them. This requires coming to know them as they are, not as we would have them be. The fact remains that each of us has a responsibility to build family relationships so that they can become life-giving. Genuine communication could solve every problem. We need to commit ourselves to this, convinced that we are basically all brothers and sisters at the Lord's table, and that the loving care of Christ is given to us all. It is all for the better if we familiarize ourselves with some of the more modern techniques of communication, whether Ginnott's being non-judgmental ("neither praise nor blame"), or Gordon's "no-lose" methods. All of these accord people the respect and dignity they deserve as brothers or sisters of Christ. That is why they work. But they are possible only when there is real love.

This brings us to the second circle, that of neighbor. This might best be imagined at the parish level. Theoretically, parishes are meant to be caring, sharing communities. They are extended families characterized by the ability to nurture their members. But, as human manifestations of this ideal, they are in fact often very imperfect. As our spiritual home they are deserving of our love, and surely in need of our concern, if they are to come closer to the ideal set by Jesus.

We cannot afford to think of the parish any longer as a spiritual service station where the parishioners are passive and all services and goods come from the top down, where *Father* is expected to do everything. Today the folly of that assumption is becoming clearer and clearer. It is the entire parish that must be a nurturing community. Any care and concern exercised by the ones in charge of the parish are meant as an example of what should be done by all.

One of the fertile fields for involvement at the parish level today is that of ecumenism. One of the sad tragedies of Christianity is that it is divided among so many competing groups. Fortunately, since the Second Vatican Council we have stopped regarding Protestant churches as intrinsically evil and begun to see them, indeed, as true churches. We should take leadership in helping to heal the divisions that have occurred over the centuries and in building those bridges that are so necessary to hasten the day when we can have that unity for which Jesus himself prayed so ardently the night before he died (Jn 17:20-23). Our concern need not always have a parish base. Our faith and love can cause us to become committed citizens of the city or place where we live. Simply because we do not have too many canonized politicians is no reason to think that these occupations are hazardous to our spiritual health. In fact, they cry our for people who are genuinely concerned about the needs of others and who are willing to spend themselves to bring about a better world. They provide fertile ground for deep Christian concern and involvement.

It is here that we enter our third circle, that of the larger world in which we live. Here also selectivity is required. It is totally impossible to concern ourselves with *all* the ills of the universe. We can, however, and *should*, choose one area, at least, where our competence or interests might direct us. There are numerous groups that keep us abreast of what is happening in national government or on a global level. Trying to influence legislation for worthwhile causes, striving to make the world more humane in whatever way we are able, giving of ourselves so that others might live decent human lives, all flow from a deeper appreciation of the meaning of communion and are manifestations of the life of the Spirit.

The ancient church used to inculcate the practice of fasting and almsgiving during Lent and at other penitential times. In truth, the two were connected. We fasted so that we might have something to give to others. This is how it was expressed in the fifth century—and in eucharistic terms—by St. Leo the Great.

> Let us now extend to the poor and those afflicted in different ways a more open-handed generosity, so that God may be thanked through many voices and the relief of the needy supported by our fasting. No act of devotion on the part of the faithful gives God more pleasure than that which is lavished on his poor. Here he finds charity with its loving concern; there he recognizes the reflection of his own fatherly care.

> In these acts of giving we need not fear a lack of means. A generous spirit is itself great wealth. There can be no shortage of material for generosity where it is Christ who feeds and Christ who is fed. In all this activity there is present the hand of him who multiplies the bread by breaking it and increases it by giving it away (Sermon 10 in *Quadragesima* 3-5; PL 54, 299-301).

The liturgy is full of reminders that we become "one body, one spirit in Christ." The commitment to nurturing growth in one another and to fostering the unity that was so dear to the heart of Christ as part of our daily life and practice requires two things. The first is the conviction that there is truly a link between liturgy and life. The privatization of religion, which served to keep it in the sanctuary and out of the marketplace, has to go the way of the horse and buggy. So intimate is this link that the quality of our Christian lives directly affects—indeed, may threaten—the fruitfulness of our eucharists. St. Paul went even further and said that the insensitive behavior of those whose hearts were closed to the poor was such a serious matter that it was not the Lord's Supper that they celebrated when they gathered (cf. 1 Cor 11:20).

The implication of the Pauline text is that the reality of our eucharistic celebrations is in a large measure conditioned by the quality of our lives. To approach the holy table with hearts and minds closed to those around us is to have them equally closed to Jesus. If we cannot recognize Christ in others, in the stranger who is in need, we will have no greater success in recognizing him in a piece of bread. Christ is not divided, and we cannot pretend to love the head without loving his entire body.

Second, we need the help of the Holy Spirit. Our ability to love others as we ourselves have been loved by Christ is dependent on both our experience of Christ's love in our lives and in the insight made possible by the Spirit into the nature of that self-giving love. Then we will realize that its application to God, neighbor, and the entire world is truly measureless. Nevertheless, it is foundational. At each eucharist Christ issues a call that his love will permeate every facet of our human living to the point where we practice a similar love for others.

Once again, as the First Letter of John tells us:

> This is the message you have heard from the beginning: we should love one another. . . . The way we came to know love was that he laid down his life for us; so we ought to lay down our lives for our brothers [and sisters]. If someone who has worldly means sees [others] in need and refuses [them] compassion, how can the love of God remain in [such a one]? Children, let us love not in word or speech but in deed and truth (1 Jn 3:11, 16-18).

In terms of the eucharistic rhythms we have been discussing, it is because we have gathered at the Lord's table and been both fed and challenged by his word to live a more authentic Christian life that we can nourish ourselves with Christ's very flesh and blood, knowing that we have received such abundance that even after we have shared there will still be far more than we could imagine left to share.

10

The Missioning Rhythm

Dance, then,
wherever you may be.
I am the Lord
of the dance, said he.
And I'll lead you all
wherever you may be.
And I'll lead you all
in the dance, said he.

Like the entrance rite, the closing ritual is not given much attention. For years we have been ending with the injunction to "go in peace," that the mass was finished, but then making valiant efforts to keep the people from leaving until we could sing a final hymn. We don't take our dismissals very seriously these days.

If we look back into our liturgical history, however, we notice that dismissals have quite a history within the mass. They have served to give us the name *mass*, which is simply an English version of the Latin *missa* ("send"). Josef A. Jungmann assures us that the final dismissal, *"Ite, missa est,"* is as old as the Roman liturgy. There is an important distinction here, in Latin anyway. We are not really saying that the mass is "ended" (*finis est*), but that it has been "accomplished" (*missa est*), and that the people are being sent forth. This is missed in translation.

We assume that dismissals belong at the end of the service. That is true. But in our mass, they have come at various other times as well. Endings came at different parts of the service, depending on who you were. We have had them at the beginning of the liturgy of the word, after the penitential rite. They have also occurred after the liturgy of the word itself. Some dismissals were just before communion. We have dismissed people at various times and for various reasons. The general rule in the early days was that those who were considered "outsiders" for various parts of the mass were dismissed at the appropriate time.

In the days of public penance, depending on what stage of reconciliation had been achieved, penitents were allowed to stay for various parts of the mass: the introduction, the liturgy of the word, even up to the communion for those in the last stages. When we had a catechumenate, the catechumens were routinely dismissed after the liturgy of the word.

At each of these moments, it was not a question of people slinking out of church at the appointed time. Rather, each group was acknowledged, given a blessing, and sent on its way with a task to fulfill. One either deepened one's spirit of penitence, or, continued the study of the scriptures and Christianity. Dismissals were a serious thing.

After the Council of Trent both the order of penitents and catechumens were a thing of the past. It was recognized that it was impractical (if not odious) to try banning public sinners from the church or to try ordering them out after the gospel. So dismissals within the liturgy passed out of existence. Now, in fact, every boundary between the church and world is broken down in our liturgical celebrations. It is no longer practicable to exclude those who are not full members of the assembly from our liturgy.

In many ways the early church was a closed society. Only those who were "children of the house" were allowed at the church's celebrations. In fact, in the fourth century not only the dismissals but also the arrivals were strictly regulated. The doors were locked for the eucharistic prayer. Those arriving late might knock and manage at least to have a prayer offered for them—that they might increase in love and zeal. That would take care of punctuality!

A remnant of this strict admission and dismissal mentality in our times is seen, in some areas, in the large number who leave the church as soon as the priest communicates. This comes from the old theology of the "important parts" of the mass. One had to stay until communion, under pain of serious sin. But for those not communicating, whether by reason of public penance or the consciousness of personal sin, it sufficed that they stay until the priest had communicated.

The only dismissal we have in the present mass comes at the end of the entire liturgy. It is obscured to a large extent by the almost universal custom of a final hymn. Instead of singing a postcommunion hymn, being dismissed with solemnity, and then leaving together to the strains of an organ postlude, people begin to drift out during the last hymn.

In some ways, everything that has preceded leads up to the final sentence of the mass: "Go in peace to love and serve the Lord." The people are not simply told to *go*. They are supposed to have been fired up to *go and serve!* The meaning of the dismissal itself is lost if more emphasis in placed on the injunction *to go*, rather than on the commission laid on all *to love and serve the Lord.*

The people are given a task, a mission. Unless this takes place, the entire liturgy is fruitless.

The rites of the eucharist make it clear that the entire liturgy is one giant sending service. People come to express their communion with each other and the Lord in order to be strengthened to live their faith more perfectly during the coming week. In the early church, long before weekday masses were a reality, Christians took home some of the consecrated bread in order to communicate during the week. It was considered important that the Sunday liturgy influence the entire week.

The ability to live one's eucharist during the week also gave the congregation something to offer the following Sunday. Thus there was the realization that one should grow from week to week and have something to bring to the altar each succeeding Sunday.

One priest used to tell people, "If you haven't been to mass during the week, don't bother coming on Sundays. You've got nothing to celebrate." He wasn't trying to foster the practice of daily mass. Rather, he was emphasizing that if people have not been active in any way in the life of the community during the week, they bring precious little to offer at the celebration on Sundays. In that he was right.

The eucharist is meant to link the liturgy of life to the liturgy of the church, and vice versa. There is a connection between what we celebrate on Sundays and what we do on Mondays. The Sunday celebration is intended to make us true members of Christ's body. That means recognizing that we have been missioned by the Lord to go forth and bear fruit.

Today it is very easy to lose the sense of being missioned. Most people assume that the only ones with responsible roles in the church are the clergy or the religious. This is natural because for years laity have been put down. We don't even have a definition for those who make up the majority in the church. The best that the Second Vatican Council and the recent *Code of Canon Law* could come up with was that laity were "neither priests nor religious." Very flattering.

This means, obviously, that those who write these documents tend to define the church around themselves. Rather than seeing clergy as being within the circle of the church, ministering to those within it, they are conceived in a more pyramidical fashion as *above* the other members of the church, defining what the church is all about. Where this obtains, the laity soon learn to keep quiet and make no waves. We have made them that way.

Consequently, people have become passive. We may joke about the "hatched, matched, and dispatched" Catholics, who see the inside of a church only three times in their lives. But over the years people have come to see the church as some sort of spiritual service station. They turn up only when they feel the need. And when they come, they come to get, not to give. Sacraments are seen as means of grace, not encounters with the Lord on life's journey.

Then there is the problem that even well-meaning people, those who are regular in participation in the church's liturgy, are often shortchanged at the eucharist. They come hungry with anticipation but leave still hungry. Perhaps the liturgy celebrated is perfunctory. Or the homily ill-prepared or nonexistent. Instead of being filled at the Lord's banquet, all they have been given are a few crumbs. Surrounded by wealth, they remain poor.

If we take the liturgy seriously, however, we realize that it is structured to empower people, not diminish them. It should make all the members aware of their gifts—and their responsibility to go forth and use them for the good of the entire church and community. Until the clergy are one in welcoming and encouraging the talents of the people, the laity may have to rely on the inner logic of the liturgy itself to keep them aware that the purpose of the eucharist is to be found in its last sentence: Go, you are missioned!

It might help us pattern ourselves on Jesus' own eucharist if we recall that it was a memorial of his own total commitment to life and to the vocation he embraced as having been given by God. It came no easier for him than for us. He had to struggle to discern what path he should walk, which direction he should take. In fact, we read in St. Luke that on the night before he died, despite his prayer, he was filled with such confusion and agony that he even sweated blood.

What did this anguish involve? Fortunately, we can reconstruct the events of that night with relative clarity. The last supper was not a peaceful and totally joyful event. During that meal Jesus was aware of the fact that Judas had agreed to betray him. His best attempts to dissuade him came to naught. Knowing that his enemies were hemming him in hung like a cloud over the entire meal. It was the hour of the powers of darkness.

As Jesus left the upper room after the supper to go back to Bethany, he paused in the garden of Gethsemane to pray and reflect on the happenings of the day. To approach the garden he would have passed countless tombs of prophets and others who had been buried there for centuries. The full paschal moon would have given the tombs a stark visibility, heightening his sense of foreboding and of death. Jesus could sense the darkness closing in on him from all sides.

As he tried to compose himself in prayer in that garden, the full reality of the situation was borne in on him with a clarity that was terrifying, making quiet prayer an impossibility. The price of commitment was strikingly clear. The injustice and seeming meaninglessness of the situation was troubling.

Jesus was wrestling with all of life's "why" questions. Why should he allow his enemies to succeed? Why remain there to let the forces of blindness triumph? What good could result from his being captured by his adversaries? Why should he suffer the indignity of being taken for a common criminal, when he had only gone about doing good? Why not disappear for a while—as he had done before—and wait for things to cool down? Perhaps then he could return and try a new approach or hope that time had softened the opposition that surrounded him. Why? Why? Why?

These were not easy questions to answer. We know what they cost Jesus even to ask. We also know that despite the agony, the blood, and his total repugnance at the thought of suffering and death, Jesus somehow felt that the Father wanted him to stay and make a stand this time. He was not simply to pass through their midst and try again elsewhere, even though it would have been easy for him to do so!

Jesus was not taken by surprise in the garden. The band of men out to capture him would have had to come down the Kidron valley, just as he had. They would have been visible in the moonlight, outlined against the walls of the Temple, even had they managed to keep quiet as they negotiated the steep slope. He saw them coming. In fifteen minutes he could have been at Lazarus's house over the hill; in a half hour the Judean desert that begins outside of Bethany could have swallowed him up. Escape was so easy! And yet he stayed. This was God's will.

In a sense Jesus had already decided this issue, present in germ in the temptations at the beginning of his public ministry. He had decided then not to use the wisdom of the world, not to seek political domination and power. He was now willing to be a suffering servant for his sisters and brothers. And so he turned his *passion* into the most free *action* the world has ever seen.

All of this is expressed in eucharist. Jesus' ability to say that the bread was his body and the wine his blood was possible because he was willing to let himself be broken and poured out for others. Life for Jesus was not a self-centered reality. Rather, he defined himself in relation to others to whom he was bound by his humanity, and he was willing to give his life for them.

If it was not easy for Jesus to offer eucharist, it should be no different for us. At each mass, when the gifts are prepared and the bread and wine are put on the paten, we thank God, the creator of all things, for having given us something to offer. We are invited to put our own lives, our hopes and our struggles, our doubts and frustrations on the paten as well. They, like the bread and wine, will be transformed during the eucharistic prayer so that they can be offered up to God as a fitting sacrifice.

Bread and wine are symbolic of our lives as well as Christ's. We lift them up at the climax of the eucharistic prayer, reminding ourselves that it is only through Christ, with him and in him, that any glory can be given to God. And we recall that—as Jesus demonstrated in the garden—transformation comes only as the result of fidelity and commitment. Eucharist makes sense solely when it represents an active concern for others.

Hence the importance of the lives we lead during the week. This is all we have to offer week by week. We place on the paten our struggles, attempts to live the faith which is ours, our efforts to be more and more faithful. Unless we have something to offer each week, we bring precious little to be transformed. Our eucharist then, instead of being a celebration of fidelity and active commitment, becomes a ritualistic exercise without personal content. This is not the eucharist of the Lord, whom we claim as our savior and brother.

In this regard, it might be good to note that Vatican II has introduced the notion of the church itself being a servant of God as well as servant of the world in memory of Christ. This whole concept of service, a key notion of Mark's gospel, is meant to be characteristic of disciples. In the final prediction of the passion, Jesus says that all those who wish to rank first must begin by being the slaves of all (Mk 10:44). Slavery carries the concept of servanthood to its ultimate limits.

Slavery in this case, however, is not the degrading reality we assume it to be. Even St. Paul defined himself as a "slave of Christ Jesus" (Rom 1:1). And Paul was not simply being humble. He was well aware the same term was used in the Old Testament of some very interesting people. First of all, it was used of Abraham, the father of the chosen people. He was called a slave of Yahweh because of his faith and fidelity.

It is also used of Abraham's son Isaac. It was through Isaac rather than Ishmael that the promises of election were transmitted. He was the son of the promise, and all have been blessed in him. Later Jewish writings depict him as a man of thirty, willingly cooperating in his own sacrifice by carrying the wood his father gave him. The lineage so far seems rather noble!

Moses was another called Yahweh's slave. He brought the people out of Egypt and led them to the promised land. His trusted lieutenant, Joshua, who actually brought them into the land, is also called a slave of Yahweh. Much later, we note that the term is applied to King David and to the prophets.

In the New Testament we have already mentioned that St. Paul called himself Jesus' slave. It is a term also used of Mary. Most translations of the annunciation have Mary say, "Behold the handmaid of the Lord," and the Magnificat reads, "He has looked on his handmaid's lowliness" (Lk 1:38, 48). The word here is the same as that used for Abraham, Moses, and David. Mary is calling herself the slave of God.

When we look at this landscape, we begin to realize that in being asked to become God's slave we are invited to join rather distinguished company. Each of these people had a key role to play in salvation history. Our willingness to become servants of the Lord—which Mark claims is an essential part of the responsibilities of discipleship—implies that we recognize the role God wants us to play in the salvation of the world.

Further, our ability to read the signs of the times should inspire us to do something about what we see. We are called to be sources of salvation, of hope, compassion, and love in a world sadly in need of these qualities. We must awaken and be touched by the pain and need of those around us. Only this will motivate us to strive actively to make this world in which we live a better and more humane place.

On a larger level, we today are required to be aware of the various ways in which we can do something to improve the social order. It is much easier to complain about the world around us than it is to become part of the solution, but complaining is nonproductive. Missioning requires that we recognize our responsibility to so live our Christianity that we make a qualitative difference in the world around us.

One way of deepening this realization at mass is to regard the dismissal for what is really is: a challenge to live what we have celebrated. Our response, "Thanks be to God," is intended to be an enthusiastic acceptance of Christ's challenge. We allow God to lead us all in his dance, wherever we may be. Each liturgy should give us a concrete challenge. We should not leave the church without having found a specific way to apply the gospel in the coming week.

A practical way of doing this would be to make better use of the reflection time after communion. We can make our thanksgiving concrete by specifying to God or to Christ how we will try to live the message of the scriptures in the days ahead. Then, when we leave the church, we will have a definite idea of how this eucharist can be effective in the redemption of the world.

As we recess out of church, we should be conscious that we have done more than fulfill an obligation. By uniting ourselves with Christ, who is both victim and priest, we have been renewed and strengthened in our resolve to live what we have celebrated more perfectly in the week ahead. We accept for a fact Jesus' words at the last supper, "Amen, amen, I say to you, whoever believes in me will do the works that I do, and will do greater ones than these, because I am going to the Father" (Jn 14:12).

11

With Open Doors: To the Ends of the Earth

Praise [God] with timbrel and dance,
praise him with strings and pipe.
Praise him with sounding cymbals. . . .
Let everything that has breath praise the Lord!
—Psalm 150:4-6

Holiness is not limited to the sanctuary or to moments of private prayer. Holiness is achieved in the midst of the world. There is an ever-recurrent temptation to want to remain with Jesus alone on Mount Tabor, to build tents and stay on the mountaintops. Like Peter, we feel that "it is good for us to be here!" Real life, however, goes on in the valleys and plains. We celebrate eucharist with the Lord in order to go forth and praise him with each daily breath.

In matters of religion the danger lies in privatizing our relationship with God. We think we are good if we manage to avoid sin and refuse to cooperate in evil. *Christian* virtue, however, requires that we consciously act out of a specific faith-conviction, as a member of a particular church. Our action is not as an isolated individual, but as part of a larger community of faith.

Pope John Paul II has recently issued a significant encyclical entitled *The Mission of the Redeemer (Redemptoris missio).* His opening words remind us that "the mission of Christ the redeemer is still very far from completion. As the second millennium after Christ's coming draws to an end, an overall view of the human race shows that this mission is still only beginning and that we must commit ourselves wholeheartedly to its service."

Lest we think that the "we" in the above sentence is meant only for the ordained or those in vows, the pope continues, "No believer in Christ . . . can avoid this supreme duty of proclaiming Christ to all peoples." Every baptized person is responsible for the mission of Christ. Eucharist is an acceptance of baptismal responsibility.

The pope lists several ways in which we can exercise this responsibility. Primary is simply basic Christian witness, which is called "the first and irreplaceable form of mission." The lives we lead are either a positive witness of our faith or an indication that we really have no faith to speak of. The church has always stressed the need to be compassionate as our Father in heaven is compassionate. In its recently articulated preferential option for the poor, it has highlighted the importance of concern for the oppressed, the downtrodden, indeed all who suffer.

Concern and generosity for the poor are a powerful witness in an individualistic age; they stand in sharp contrast to the selfishness of a materialistic society. The ability to provide such witness "raises questions [in people's minds] that leads to God and to the gospel." The counter-witness of an authentically Christian life is always effective witness.

This is only natural. The important questions of life are not philosophical ones for most people; they are gut questions. People do not want to have it proven to them that Christianity is revealed by God and is the best possible religion. They want to see it demonstrated concretely in people's lives. Whether Christianity is the answer to human needs will depend on how it is lived. As the pope notes, "People today put more faith in witnesses than in teachers, in experience than in teaching, and in life and action than in theories."

This witness is not always a quiet one. Depending on where we live or work, or how we are situated, we are at times required to go further. In the pope's own words, we may need to take a "courageous and prophetic stand in the face of the corruption of political or economic power." We cannot fall back on the "everybody's doing it" excuse. "A commitment to peace, justice, human rights and human promotion is also a witness to the gospel when it is a sign of concern for persons and is directed towards integral human development."

After the witness of example, there is a second level of witness: the initial proclamation of Christ. As the pope puts it, "The church cannot elude Christ's explicit mandate [to preach the good news to the ends of the earth] nor deprive men and women of the 'good news' about their being loved and saved by God."

This underscores a basic truth. The church itself is essentially missionary. It is not the pope or any bishop or priest who missions people. The church is not the sender; it is the one sent. It exists only in being sent and in building itself up for the sake of its mission. Because we have a missionary God we are a missionary people.

As one good Protestant bishop put it, the church is the only society in the world that exists for the sake of those who are not its members. This is a striking way of putting the insight of Vatican II, which opens its constitution *The Church in the Modern World* with the sentence, "The joys and hopes, the grief and anguish of the people of our time, especially of those who are poor or afflicted in any way, are the joys and hopes, the grief and anguish of the followers of Christ as well."

In this sense, the world sets the agenda for the church. We cannot close our eyes to the needs of the world around us. Here is where our prayer and worship help us to maintain a sensitivity to the needs of others. In prayer we enter into the heart of Christ, acknowledging and celebrating the source of our life. The final rhythm of this prayer, however, sends us out to share what we are and what we have received with those around us.

We might call this responsibility *involvement*. We gather in Christ's name to hear his word and be strengthened to go forth as the light of the world, as the salt that gives savor. It follows that we will have something to offer the world only if we remain different from it. Christians must maintain a conscious uniqueness in order to become "the experimental garden of the new humanity."

The vision of re-creation that this suggests is appropriate. It is akin to the prophetic vision of Isaiah, who spoke of messianic times as inaugurating that era when the lion and the lamb could lie together in peace, when children could play with venomous snakes, and where all would be one harmonious garden. He thought in terms of a new Eden. Mission, in this sense, is God's desire to save and grace the entire world. It is the reason for the incarnation.

In Vatican II's constitution *The Church in the Modern World* this global understanding of mission is treated in terms of the action of the Holy Spirit. The history of the world is not only the story of evil; it is the history of

God's reign being advanced by the work of the Spirit. "The Spirit of God . . . with marvelous providence directs the unfolding of time and renews the face of the earth." This is close to the Pauline vision of Romans 8:18-27, where creation itself is said to be longing for that redemption which the Spirit can bring.

This takes us beyond a tendency to subsume all mission and grace under the work of Christ. A narrow focus on Jesus tends to leave out the Holy Spirit. It is important that we keep this in mind as we face the tasks that lie ahead in the third millennium. We may see the Holy Spirit as having been released by Christ; nevertheless, the work of the Spirit goes beyond the ordinary vision of the church and is not confined to any institution. We know that the Spirit blows where she wills. But if we are attuned to her workings, we need not fear being narrowly sectarian in our efforts to bring about that more integral vision of a world where all can live in peace and harmony.

That is surely the vision that inspired Isaiah. It is likewise the one that inspired Jesus, as we see in his inaugural sermon in his home town (Lk 4:16-30). Then he used Isaiah as a starting point, proclaiming that the Spirit had anointed him to bring the good news to the poor, to proclaim liberty to captives and recovery of sight to the blind, to let the oppressed go free. The work of the Spirit is bigger than we are, or than our vision can ever comprehend.

It is possible to read Luke in such a way that it is seen as the lonely struggle of one man against everyone else in Nazareth. Jesus was surely inspired with the Isaian vision of restoration; his desire to bring about a renewed Israel was shaped by previous prophetic longings. Nevertheless, when Jesus said that the Spirit of the

Lord was upon him, he never meant to imply that the Spirit was his alone! He was not there to announce that he was the one-man show who would single-handedly bring about what generations of people had longed for.

Rather, Jesus was doing in Nazareth what we see him doing in so many other gospel passages as he began his public ministry: looking for help. The gospels all attest that Jesus began his work by associating disciples with himself. Jesus' call was not a self-proclamation as much as it was an effort to inspire others as he himself had been inspired by the Isaian challenge. If others could be fired with the same vision, together it could be brought closer to completion.

Jesus' problem in Nazareth is the same as that which we find in many Christian churches today. People are willing to have Jesus as part of their lives as long as he has something to give them. "Do here in your native place the things that we heard were done in Capernaum" (Lk 4:23). We are glad to acknowledge Jesus as one of us so long as we can sit back and profit from his mercy and love. Religion is fine as long as we benefit, but when it asks us to disturb ourselves to bring benefits to others, we back off. Jesus was offering this second kind of challenge. He was saying that he had not come to set up shop in one place for one people, but to enlist them in his crusade to transform the whole of society.

When we accept Jesus' invitation to share at his table we are, in fact, accepting a solidarity with him that goes far beyond the Nazarenes' excited "He is one of us!" (cf. 4:22). Implied is an assent to Jesus' challenge and a willingness to say, "We are one with him!" Accepting solidarity with Christ means accepting his vision; it proclaims that we are equally inspired by it and wish to make it our own. Thus we gather to hear his word week after week, so that we might be challenged and strengthened to take our expected places in the transformation of the society in which we live. To attempt anything less, to take only what we can get for ourselves, is to accept Christ's invitation deceitfully.

It is important that we keep alive this vision of what Jesus called the kingdom. For it is this vision that will enable us to know what needs to be done in any given time and place to help bring the kingdom about. A vision keeps us pointed in the right direction, enabling us to maintain our purpose and steer the right course amid competing visions and ideologies. A vision is larger than we are, so it is able to inspire us throughout life. It is larger, even, than the church, and thus it attunes us to see and appreciate the action of the Holy Spirit in the world in anything that is good and noble or that leads to the community of humanity that the church tries to model. We should never forget that our God is a God of surprises. As Paul told the Philippians, "Finally . . . whatever is true, whatever is honorable, whatever is just, whatever is pure, whatever is lovely, whatever is gracious, if there is any excellence and if there is anything worthy of praise, think about these things" (Phil 4:8).

Theologically, the concept of an active and missioned church is based on solid and ancient theology. Vatican II saw fit to resurrect the biblical and patristic teaching on the common priesthood of all believers. This anchors the conciliar teaching that all the baptized by reason of baptism have equal dignity, an equal call to holiness, and an equal responsibility for the work of the gospel. Thus any ministry done by members of the church is not to be considered an extension of the work of the hierarchy as much as something that flows from our common baptism. Ministry does not belong to the hierarchy by right; theirs is only a particularized ministry within the Christian community.

The scripture passages that speak of our being a royal priesthood come from 1 Peter and the Book of Revelation. 1 Peter, especially, offers a well-thought-out baptismal theology. The point of the message is clear and simple: the task of faithful discipleship is not to flee the world but to participate in it. In a bold missionary thrust, Christians are challenged to lead the world to the praise of God.

What we have here is a *witness* spirituality. The example of Christian love and service that builds the community is the most powerful message we can give a world starved for meaning. Our life-witness can change the world. This is the Christian vocation. The letter was written to remind the baptized that we are united in baptism in order to exercise discipleship in the midst of the world.

The author insists on two things. The first is that all are called to be active participants in the structures of the world. The author fully expects the faithful and committed lives of Christians to be a force for the conversion of others. Only by living the Christian life fully in the midst of the world can we further the work of God, who is working in and though us to move the world to its destiny, that is, to the fullness of the redemption brought by Christ. Second, the author realizes that if Christians are to live with integrity and in strength, destructive passions must be let go and our eyes kept fixed on Christ, who has loved us and given his life for us. Ultimately, we must develop the courage to live the vocation to which each of us is called. This is still important advice today.

Likewise, when 1 Peter speaks of "spiritual" sacrifices, this is to be taken in the light of the contrast between *flesh* and *spirit* so often used by St. Paul. Every action and sacrifice that is pleasing to God is spiritual and utterly real (cf. Rom 12:1). As St. Augustine put it, "The true offering consists of every act we make with the intention of uniting with God in a holy and living communion."

The message of Revelation is the same. Stated in more liturgical terms, we are reminded that the reign of God will be brought about through victory over the world of sin. We are not subjects, but rulers together with Christ. John looks to the eschatological fulfillment of the kingdom for which Jesus lived and died. More than 1 Peter, he sketches a vision of a eucharistic community gathered together for the praise and glory of God, aware of its dignity and living up to its privileges and responsibilities.

The breviary for Wednesday of the fifth week of Easter has an excerpt from a Letter to Diognetus. Further excerpted, we have the following witness, which is worth pondering:

> Christians are indistinguishable from others either by nationality, language or customs. They do not inhabit separate cities of their own, or speak a strange dialect, or follow some outlandish way of life. Unlike other people they champion no purely human doctrine. With regard to dress, food and manner of life in general, they follow the customs of whatever city they happen to be living in, whether it is Greek or foreign.

And yet, there is something extraordinary about their lives. They live in their own countries as though they were only passing through. They play their full role as citizens, but labor under the disabilities of aliens. . . . To speak in general terms, we may say that the Christian is to the world what the soul is to the body. As the soul is present in every part of the body, while remaining distinct from it, so Christians are found in all cities of the world, but cannot be identified with the world.

It would seem that we are once again beginning to experience the vitality described in this early Christian letter. Surely one of the most dramatic shifts taking place in the church today is the movement away from seeing ministry or apostolate as the monopoly of the ordained to seeing it more and more (and rightly so) as the responsibility of all the baptized. Some have even referred to this "laicization" of the church as marking the end of the Constantinian church. Long may it rest in peace.

Vatican II accepted this shift, at least in theory. In *Lumen gentium* we read that "the apostolate of the laity is sharing in the salvific mission of the church. Through baptism and confirmation, all are appointed to this apostolate by the Lord himself" (no. 33). *Ad gentes* goes even further and states categorically that "the church is not fully established and does not fully live, nor is it a perfect sign of Christ, unless there is a genuine laity existing and working alongside the hierarchy" (no. 21).

In the church, the most striking example of vitality and of lay ministry in recent years has been in the phenomenon of the base Christian communities (BCC) or basic ecclesial communities. Having begun in Latin

America, they are now spread over the globe. In the Philippines they make it possible for the church to survive in a country where there is a desperate shortage of priests. This has brought about a sense of dignity and empowerment to people who previously thought of themselves as of little worth.

Though base Christian communities seem to fare better in third-world countries or in rural areas, the idea is beginning to take hold even in the urbanized Western world. Various efforts to break large parishes into smaller units are all traceable to the experience of the BCCs. In many cases these are geographically based, but they can also begin as prayer groups or Bible study groups. Some charismatic groups have even banded together as covenanted communities.

In each case small groups of committed Christians meet and take responsibility for their own faith and for its spread in the world in which we live. Experience shows the importance of having other Christians with whom we can pray and find the encouragement to grow in the resolve to be the salt of the earth and the light of the world. In such small groups we can reflect communally on the scriptures and take seriously the responsibility to live our faith to the full in the world today.

Ultimately, mission is a multifaceted reality involving everyone in the church in witness, service to others, justice, healing, reconciliation, peace, fellowship, ecumenism, and whatever it takes to build the kingdom. Many of these aspects have been mentioned only in passing in this book. Where we place the emphasis may well depend on how we understand Jesus, and where we place the importance in the gospel story.

Today, many people give increased importance to the *incarnation*. Taking the humanity of Jesus more seriously, for example, has been the approach of liberation theology and of the BCCs. This approach focuses on the actual practice of Jesus in his own lifetime. The Western colonialist church has been accused justly of having focused so much on the divinity of Christ that it was unable to take the very option for the poor that Jesus himself did.

There has been a preoccupation with the *cross* in Christian life since the days of Anselm. Unfortunately, this was often separated from the life of Christ. The gift of self that characterizes Jesus began at his birth and is evidenced in his public life as well as his crucifixion. Nevertheless, it remains true that the cross does stand for reconciliation of people who are alienated from one another. It demands sacrifices from both oppressors and oppressed. We have to learn to love our enemies the way that Jesus did, or any work for the kingdom will come to naught.

In the Eastern churches, especially, it is the *resurrection* that is seen as the salvific event par excellence. In recent years we in the West have begun to pay added attention to its significance. Instead of exclusive focus on the cross, we are careful to say that we were saved by the life, death, and resurrection of Christ. On a practical level, this means that our lives should proclaim the risen Christ. We are all called to live a risen life in the world today as a sign of contradiction against the forces of death and destruction, unmasking modern idols and false absolutes.

In this ecumenical age the Calvinist tradition would have us add the *ascension* to the above trilogy. Though associated with Easter by John, it is stressed by Matthew and Luke as a separate event. At any rate, it enables us to see ourselves as living in the time of the church, between the ascension and the *parousia*. And it helps us to look back at the cross and see it as the beginning of the consummation of the ages. From a practical point of view, it prevents us from developing a disincarnate spirituality in which we refuse to involve ourselves in the world that must be brought to fulfillment (cf. Rom 8:18-25).

Pentecost is another important moment; it puts the focus on the presence of the Holy Spirit in the church. We have long ignored the presence and action of the Spirit in the church. In recent years the charismatic movement has reminded us of this lack. Some of the criticisms made of the charismatics is that they seem to have paid little attention to the reality of the cross. Nevertheless, they provide a needed reminder of the importance of a church in which the gifts of the Spirit are in evidence, and where all care for one another.

Finally, some emphasize the *parousia*. There are a number of groups, often associated with Protestant fundamentalists, who place much attention on the final coming of Christ. Emphasis on judgment or the final coming has never been that strong in the Catholic tradition. However, we need to be reminded that the future is important, if only to provide a needed vision of the coming triumph of good over the forces of evil. Such a focus also prevents us from identifying the church with the kingdom, allowing us to critique it and to see it as the vanguard of God's reign, of the new heavens and the new earth to which we can all look forward.

None of these approaches can be profitably understood in isolation or exclusion. All are needed if the gospel message is not to be not to be truncated and denatured. But one or another tends to predominate, depending on a person's theological predilections.

Here we have tried to cut across this theological spectrum in order to provide a eucharistic paradigm for Christian life, which in many ways ranges across each of the above emphases. Because the liturgical year focuses on each of the various mysteries of Christian faith in turn, it provides over the course of the year a holistic expression of the mystery of salvation and of our incorporation in Christ.

It is important to realize and maintain this perspective. By stressing the rhythms of the eucharist celebration itself, our claim is that they not only dictate to us the basic rhythms of Christian life itself, but that the celebration of eucharist is directly affected by how its rhythms are lived out in the lives of the Christians who gather for worship. We cannot claim to be Christian if we reduce prayer and worship to some sacred realm which is not at the same time grounded in the very profane reality of our everyday lives.

Of all the rhythms, that of missioning is the one most easily neglected. We have been brought up to think that all God wanted of us was that we avoid sin. But if our lives are to reflect the cosmic dance of God, accepting Christ's invitation to dine at his table expresses a willingness to become his instrument, his missionary, in the salvation of the world.

12

After the Dance

Many religions have holy places, holy things, holy people. Is this good? It can be a problem if it creates a gap between the realm of the profane and that of the holy. Then the holy gets progressively reduced to only a fraction of one's life. This leads to the compartmentalization of religion. Consequently the world is relegated to a neutral place or, even worse, a place of evil, belonging to Satan. The world, somehow, has nothing to do with religion.

The incarnation of Jesus should convince Christians that the holy is not separate from the profane. By taking up human flesh to live as all of us must, Jesus revealed the possibility of sanctifying the whole of life and glorifying God in our daily activities. Jesus lived a very profane life in one sense. He was not a sacred person. He never ministered in the Temple. His ministry was concerned with the everyday activities of the people he met. And he died on a rock pile outside the city as a victim of state execution. Not very holy.

Jesus' life redefines what holiness is all about. In a sense, Christianity has shifted the idea of holiness from things, or actions, to history—to time itself. The "day of the Lord" that is often mentioned in prophetic literature has many echoes in the New Testament as well. Learning to sanctify God's day, to hallow time, is more important than searching out the Lord in a holy house. In fact, what we do in the Lord's house is meant to enable us to do a better job of investing all our days with the imprint of their creator.

Jewish tradition put enormous emphasis on keeping holy the Sabbath. This was what distinguished the Jews from other nations. The idea of sabbath rest was part and parcel of their thinking. It guaranteed their covenant relationship with God and made them pleasing to him. Despite this fact, the early Christians put more emphasis on Sunday than the sabbath. Strange!

This was not simply a question of shifting the holy day to a more convenient time. There was a whole new theology involved. If the sabbath was a day of rest, Sunday was a day of work. Just as God began the work of creation on the first day, so did he begin the work of re-creation on that same day. The day of the resurrection was the one when Christians gathered in order to commit themselves to Christ's own work of redemption, to go out and inspire themselves to transform time, all of history, with the leaven of the gospel.

A special consciousness is required to recognize the ultimate significance of time. We all live in it, but it is so much a part of our lives that we often fail to notice it. However, human existence is ultimately explicable only by understanding time, God's time, so that we can understand his plan for humanity.

Creation is the language of God. Time is his music, his dance, and creation is called to share in that dance. Our Sunday liturgies are means of entering into the rhythm of God, of becoming masters of our space in order to sanctify time and be sanctified by it. This is how God teaches us to walk—or dance—as his children. This is how all of life is truly made holy.

No matter how well or how poorly celebrated the liturgy is, it contains a wealth of symbolism. This symbolism has the power to transform our human experience by giving meaning to the various events that make up our daily lives. The enormity of this task can be seen from the tremendously dissimilar experiences and different needs of the people in any congregation. They come from a variety of ages and backgrounds and are at diverse levels as regards growth in faith. Somehow the liturgy is expected to meet the needs of all who gather and help them hallow their lives.

Liturgy accomplishes this because its symbolic wealth can speak to people at various points along the spectrum. It deals with a reality so rich that we can take from it what we need and what we are prepared to understand. But always it invites us to go deeper, to enter more fully into the mystery of Christ, into God's dance, to make our lives Christian in the fullest sense of that term.

We should not discount the cumulative effect of regular Sunday eucharists. Our hope is that years of eucharistic celebration will leave their mark by helping people form pervasive attitudes about life's meaning and grow somehow in faith and love. This is the liturgy's direct, even if long-term, effect. The celebrations themselves, when experienced over time, are able to mold attitudes, to shape values, to make Christians out of those who come to share them. The liturgy, in a sense, offers a deeper experience of reality than we gain from everyday life. As the gift of a loving God, it uncovers for us the meaning of all created reality.

Thus, what we *do* Sunday after Sunday is not primarily something we offer to God, but actions which sustain us, empower us, and slowly transform us.

Sacred time (in the liturgical action) and linear time (in our daily lives) become one through the renewal of Jesus' words and actions in the liturgical cycle. Gradually, we are taken up into God's time and way of looking at things, and we deepen within ourselves the realization that the eucharist encapsulates the meaning of Christian life. The eucharist, as Vatican II has reminded us, is the source of Christian life.

But as Edward Kilmartin has noted often, this liturgical view of the meaning of human existence is only plausible and credible to the extent that it actually becomes the orientating center and source of power for the activity of Christians in all spheres of life. There is nothing magical or automatic about the eucharist. The days when we felt that as long as we were not in the state of mortal sin we would receive a superabundance of grace simply for being there are gone forever. The liturgy has to be seen for what it actually is: an interpersonal relationship offered us by Christ, a relationship that requires an equal fullness of presence on our part to be fruitful.

Eucharist, however, is not only the source but also the summit of Christian life. In a way, it is a celebration of the reality of our lives. This is frightening; it tells us that our daily life makes a real difference. The faith or lack of faith we bring to the celebration, the depth of commitment that is ours, the example of Christianity that we embody—all of these affect the liturgy that we celebrate. We cannot offer lives in total opposition to what the liturgy symbolizes and expect that liturgy to be graced for us.

Fortunately, at most liturgies the congregation is made up of a variety of peoples, most of whom would very much like to profit from their time with the risen

Christ. They have been conditioned to think of the eucharist as the ultimate sacramental expression of the church, even if they do not much understand it, or may be terribly bored by it all. Nevertheless, Christ is able to make something of whatever good will they exhibit.

Thinking of the liturgy in terms of its basic rhythms rather than in the categories of sacrifice, real presence, and communion, or liturgy of the word and liturgy of the eucharist, is not to ignore these distinctions, but to try to situate them in a new framework. The older theology does not excite or transform people. If the eucharist is to be truly the orienting center for a new life, it has to be seen as an actual reflection of what Christian life is all about.

Christ's real presence in the eucharist is often understood in a very passive way, as some sort of static physical presence. Our task at liturgy is not to be there as passive spectators but to appreciate and respond to what is being celebrated. At eucharist, we need to recognize the Christ who is present there, not only in the consecrated bread and wine, but in the assembly gathered in his name, in the word which is proclaimed, in the priest who presides, and in the charity that should characterize the community. The presence of Christ overwhelms us with its pervasiveness and power. Unless we appreciate this, we cannot respond with a faith and love that will transform us.

The rhythms of the eucharist are more than an allegorical way of interpreting the mass. They represent the overall flow of the liturgical action. They also correspond to what should be the flow of Christian life itself and what it means to be a member of the church. Thus we can gain deeper insight into the Christian reality of our lives by better understanding the meaning and movement of the mass. Further, the closer our life rhythms are to those of the eucharist, the more fruitful will the celebration be.

The centrality of the gathering rhythm corresponds to the nature of the church itself as the body of Christ, the community that gathers in memory of him to continue his work on earth. A greater attention to the meaning of this aspect of the eucharist will give us a far better appreciation for what it means to be redeemed. It is also a reflection of the inner life of God himself. Even though these trinitarian perspectives have only been hinted at, they pervade and ground any communitarian understanding of liturgy and church.

This can also be seen in the two closely linked rhythms of storytelling and prophesying. Christians must live from God's revelation. Our religion is not self-centered, but something we have received from the Father through Christ Jesus. It is rooted in the word of God, just as our lives must be if they are to remain Christian. But this word, as the Letter to the Hebrews tells us, is living and effective, "sharper than any two-edged sword . . . able to discern reflections and thoughts of the heart" (4:12) More than being simply informative, inspirational, or consoling, it is challenging, urging us to the fullness of life in Christ which the Spirit inspires.

The importance of the nurturing rhythm is obvious in the liturgy. It is the culmination of the entire ritual. Jesus has invited us to his table and nourished us with his word and with his flesh and blood. He fills us with himself so that we might fill others as well. The more our daily lives consciously reflect this concern and compassion of God, the more will we be able to enter into the heart of Christ at eucharist. Entrance is guaranteed if we allow the Spirit to help us recognize Jesus in the poor and the oppressed, the marginalized of the world, the very segment of society with which Jesus himself most closely identified.

Likewise, for the missioning rhythm. This element was almost forgotten, at least for the laity. But since the Second Vatican Council we have come to see that the gifts of the Spirit are in the entire church, not only its hierarchy. Further, we see the church itself not so much as missioned, but as a living mission in and to the world. The church does not exist for itself, but rather to bring the light of Christ to the nations.

To a great extent the eucharist involves us in the tension that will always exist between God's saving actions in the past, especially as seen in Jesus, and the as yet unfulfilled promise of redemption that will be ours at the *parousia*. Liturgy gives us the opportunity to reconnect our present selves to what we have been and to what we can become. It is this promise of the future that should keep us open to the action of the Holy Spirit in our lives.

By situating us squarely in the center of God's saving actions, we can range back over what God has done, knowing that his saving power is still operative through the sacrament. We also look forward, aware that each time we celebrate we proclaim the death of the Lord "until he comes again." That forward look to the yet unfulfilled future is important. It keeps us from complacency, from thinking that all is well, and from assuming that progress has come to an end. It helps us measure the "what is" against the "what should be."

For a book which takes an essentially liturgical approach to the eucharist, we have studiously avoided overt references to words beloved of liturgists—such as *anamnesis, epiclesis, eschatology,* and the like—though the reality behind these expressions has been developed. More seriously, it may even seem that almost no attention has been given the most central element of the liturgy itself: the eucharistic prayer. Do not the rhythms place all the stress of the liturgy of the word, the communion rite, and the dismissal, to the neglect of what we have always considered to be the heart of the action?

It might take another book to analyze this, but the approach followed here is based on the assumption that the basic structure of the mass is that of a fraternal meal, one shared by the Christian community with its risen Savior. As such, the most obvious actions are precisely those of gathering the community together, telling the stories, feeding them, and sending them home again. That is a structure that goes back to the last supper. It is more primitive and basic than the present structure or the exact content of any of its parts.

What should be avoided in any use of the rhythms approach is an overly literal application of any rhythm to only one particular section of the mass. The storytelling rhythm, for example, is not tied to the liturgy of the word and only to the liturgy of the word. We have the heart of our myth, our story, situated in the center of the eucharistic prayer itself in the words of institution. Likewise the prophetic rhythm is reinforced in the eucharistic prayer when we pray that the Holy Spirit transform not only the gifts, but us as well, so that we truly become what we claim to be: the body of Christ Jesus.

In the same way, the missioning dimension is not restricted to the last sentence of the liturgy! Again, the eucharistic prayer reminds us that what we are doing is "in memory of" Christ, Christ who is not separated from the Father and the Spirit. This same Christ is somehow present in a real and profound way in history in the ecclesial body which is rooted in and nourished by his eucharistic body. The missionary aspect of the church is rooted in its trinitarian origin.

The eucharistic prayer, far from being peripheral to the overall rhythms, gives us the spirit of thanksgiving, which should pervade the entire celebration. It deals with the saving actions of Christ, which provide the model of sacrificial life that is the pattern for all authentic Christian life.

The fact remains that a major emphasis of the book is on the presence of Christ in the church, and the community dimension of our liturgical celebrations. For this no apology is needed. It is an emphasis too long neglected in favor of an individualistic piety, which helped reduce the mass to a narrow focus on what happens to the bread and wine. The main emphasis should be on what happens to *people* who share bread and wine in memory of Christ. This was the primary focus of the early church.

In our present eucharistic prayers we have become used to a split *epiclesis*. That is, we call upon the Holy Spirit before the words of institution to transform the gifts that they might become the body and blood of our Lord Jesus Christ. After the memorial prayer we resume and ask her to transform the community into Christ's true body. Interestingly, many of the early epicleses were only for the transformation of the community. It was taken for granted that the bread and wine had to be transformed in order to bring about a change in the community, whose deification even (for some of the Eastern Fathers) came about through union with the Spirit-filled flesh of Christ.

We have not always stressed the role of the Holy Spirit as much as we would have liked. This might be a weakness in view of the fact that in the Western church we have tended to see the eucharist essentially from a christological perspective. That is, we see the eucharist as geared primarily to bringing about the intimate real presence of Christ in the host—to the neglect of the other ways in which Jesus is likewise present to us.

Once again, however, the emphasis on the presence of Christ in the community can be seen as a plea for a recognition of the role of the Holy Spirit. For it is the Spirit who constitutes the church and makes possible Christ's presence within it. The life of the church itself, as Yves Congar has noted, is one long epiclesis.

"Do this in memory of me." This is really the heart of the eucharist. Yet to do something in memory of Jesus means that we must feel, act, think, and love in such a way that Jesus is recognizable in us. Remembering takes place because of the witness provided by the assembly, both for itself and for the world. This is a collective action, one in which we help each other to become what God's grace offers to each of us whenever we gather in memory of Christ.

Each time we celebrate the memorial of Christ's passover, we enter into the continuing work of our salvation. This is a cooperative venture. In the varied rhythms of the eucharist the Lord reveals to us the presence of sin in our selfishness, in our apathy or complicity in injustice, while drawing us toward a new life. Through the sharing in his body and blood we are progressively wrenched from the forces of evil. In this same movement we match our steps to those of God himself and offer to the Father our own lives along with the hopes and sufferings of all those with whom we are working to build a society based on justice and love. He is the Lord of the dance.